MAN ON THE RUN

HELPING HYPER-HOBBIED MEN RECOGNIZE THE BEST THINGS IN LIFE

| Zeke Pipher |

HOWARD BOOKS
A DIVISION OF SIMON & SCHUSTER, INC.
New York   Nashville   London   Toronto   Sydney   New Delhi

Howard Books
A Division of Simon & Schuster, Inc.
1230 Avenue of the Americas
New York, NY 10020

Copyright © 2012 by Ezekiel Pipher

First Howard Books trade paperback edition March 2012

HOWARD and colophon are trademarks of Simon & Schuster, Inc.

For information about special discounts for bulk purchases,
please contact Simon & Schuster Special Sales at
1–866–506–1949 or business@simonandschuster.com

The Simon & Schuster Speakers Bureau can bring authors to your
live event. For more information or to book an event contact the
Simon & Schuster Speakers Bureau at 1–866–248–3049 or
visit our website at www.simonspeakers.com.

Designed by Julie Schroeder

Manufactured in the United States of America

10 9 8 7 6 5 4 3 2 1

Library of Congress Cataloging-in-Publication Data
Pipher, Ezekiel Bray.
Man on the run : helping hyper-hobbied men recognize the best things /
Ezekiel Bray Pipher.
    p. cm
Includes bibliographical references.
Designed by Julie Schroeder
ISBN 978–1–4516–1721–4
1. Men—Conduct of life. 2. Values. 3. Hobbies—Psychological aspects.
4. Interest (Psychology) 5. Spiritual life. I. title.
BJ1601.P67 2012
155.3'329—dc23
2011035919

ISBN 978–1–4516–1721–4
ISBN 978–1–4516–1722–1 (ebook)

For Jamie, my true companion

CONTENTS

Acknowledgments   ix

Introduction: The Finish Line   1

1   MAN OVERBOARD   7

2   RUNNING TOWARD, RUNNING FROM   21

3   WHEN PASSIONS CAUSE PAIN   39

4   BROKEN OUT OF THE BOX   49

5   THE CHEERING VOICE   61

6   AN INTERNAL COMPASS   79

7   THE FAMILIAR TOUCH
OF THE LONG-MARRIED   95

8   MONKEYS AT THE ZOO   109

9   STRONG, TALL CEDARS   127

10   THE DAMNABLY DIFFICULT ADVENTURE   145

11   FULLY HERE NOW   161

CONTENTS

<u>12</u> TOUCH POINTS WITH THE UNTAMED 177

<u>13</u> MAKING OTHERS GREAT 195

<u>14</u> DRIVEN BY DREAMS 209

Endnotes 223

Author Questionnaire 227

ACKNOWLEDGMENTS

Man on the Run could not have been written apart from my friends who let me tell their stories. I'd like to express a special word of thanks to Jeff Brehm, RB Drickey, Bryan Clark, Thom Ludtke, Scott Westlund, Nathan Musgrave, J. J. Springer, Larry Myers, Mike Toukan, Scott Johnson, Mike Husman, Mark McHargue, Brandon Hamer, Brian Buhlke, Richard Wischmeier, Matt Green, Dan Bailey, Tom Osborne, Steve Chapman, Charlie Alsheimer, Brett Strait, and my pastoral cluster for your input into my life and this book. Thanks also to Christian Berg, Dan Schmidt, and Joe Bell. I enjoy our partnership in the world of outdoor writing.

Thanks to my mother, Mary Pipher, for introducing me to the world of words. You continue to be the perfect writing companion. I'm extremely thankful to my agent, Rachelle Gardner, for challenging and expanding my vision for this work. I'm also grateful to the elders at Heartland Evangelical Free Church for giving me the time to complete this book.

I am deeply indebted to all my editors and readers— Jamie Pipher, Mary Pipher, Jim Pipher, Rachelle Gardner, Andy Meisenheimer, Philis Boultinghouse, Nathan Musgrave, Sandy

Musgrave, Matt Green, Mindi Green, J. J. Springer, Mary Craig, Bev Drickey, and Karmen Hamer. Your feedback not only improved my writing, it helped form my ideas. Thanks to one of my favorite pastor-scholars, Bryan Clark, for your theological critique.

I'd like to express a special love and appreciation to three of my favorite people in the world: my children, Kate, Aidan, and Claire. You bring an inexpressible amount of joy to my life, and God continues to use each of you to open my eyes to the important things in life.

My deepest gratitude belongs to my wife. As I wrote, Jamie, more than anyone else, encouraged, challenged, and cheered me on.

MAN ON THE RUN

Will I always feel this way, so empty, so estranged?

—RAY LAMONTAGNE, "EMPTY"

INTRODUCTION:
THE FINISH LINE

Two years ago, I walked with a sportsman to the end of his life. Dale died slowly of a painful disease, which provided us with several opportunities to talk before he took his last breath. We met in his small apartment. He'd sit in his faded brown recliner, and I'd pull a folding chair away from the kitchen table and position it in front of him. Usually, our conversations lasted about an hour, then Dale would get tired, and we'd call it a day.

During our times together, Dale would return to the same two topics. The first was his love for hunting and fishing. Since he'd been a boy, he had spent every possible moment outside, either on a lake or in a deer stand. On his bedside table, he had an old leather photo album with "Memories" stitched into the cover. The pages displayed photo after photo of Dale holding stringers of fish, kneeling by rows of pheasants, or standing beside deer hanging from trees. From our first meeting, it was clear that Dale and I shared the same passion for the outdoors.

When he recalled his adventures, his cheeks glowed like a young boy's.

But the enthusiasm Dale exhibited when he told his hunting and fishing stories would disappear when we moved on to our second topic: his relationships and other commitments. His glow would be replaced with ponderous sorrow. He'd slump down into his recliner. His voice would take on a somber tone, and he'd say over and over again something along the lines of, "I blew it, Pastor. I absolutely blew it!"

Dale was haunted by his memories. For every story of a successful outdoor adventure, he had three stories of missed opportunities as a husband, father, or friend. He'd put his hunting and fishing ahead of school plays, ballet recitals, and football games. He'd taken trips with buddies when he should have been on vacations with his family. He'd spent too much money on rifle shells and fishing lures and not enough on his wife and kids. His pursuit of the next outdoor thrill trumped his more important commitments. In his final days, this realization tormented him.

About five weeks before Dale's death, we had one of our last conversations. He was lying in his recliner, hooked up to oxygen. He'd lost more weight than he could afford to lose, and his bony frame seemed almost to disappear in that large, pillowy chair. We'd talked about hunting and fishing for a few moments. He'd wanted to hear about my luck that hunting season. Then, as always, the conversation turned. Dale stared out the window for a few minutes. A tear dripped from his bottom eyelash. He asked, "Will these feelings of shame stick with me until I die?"

The question caught me off guard. He deserved the truth, and I didn't know it. There was a moment of silence, and then I put my hand on the paper-thin skin of his forearm and said, "I don't know, Dale. I really hope not."

He never lost his shame. The last time I visited him, two weeks before his death, he told me that he'd give anything to go back and get a do-over on life.

Dale's funeral was on a cloudy, gray Saturday in January. As I drove home from the church, my conscience felt sore and irritated. Funerals always make me reflective, but Dale's service hit me especially hard. I'd just wrapped up an ambitious hunting season, the type of season in which I had crossed lines and apologized multiple times. I'd vowed to myself that I'd hunt no more than twice a week but found ways to stretch that number to three or four. I knew I was overdoing it when my kids started asking me each morning, "Are you hunting *again* today, Daddy?"

Far too often that season, my answer was, "Yeah . . . I think so."

Dale's tragic finish made a strong impression on me. At the time of his funeral, I'd been married for twelve years to Jamie, a patient, long-suffering woman. We had three young children, who fastened themselves to me from the moment I returned home from work until I scooped them up for a bedtime story. I was in my fourth year as a senior pastor. I was thirty-seven years old, and many potentially regret-filled chapters of my life still lay in front of me.

I didn't want *those* chapters to be written.

Jonathan Edwards once resolved, "that I will live so, as I shall wish I had done when I come to die." After the funeral, nothing seemed more important than finishing life without regrets. I didn't want my conscience nagging at me at my finish line, reminding me that I could have been a better man. I wanted to figure out how I could enjoy my many pursuits without losing sight of what matters most in life.

Men need to be alive inside. As a pastor, I spend several hours a week counseling pursuit-driven, ambitious men. In just the past week, I worked with a man who spends too much time researching and buying wine, another man who hunts ducks five mornings a week, and a man in his fifties who watches thirty-five hours of television every week. If there's one theme in my pastoral ministry and counseling, it's that men are easily knocked off balance and into trouble.

But it doesn't need to be this way. Men can live well. *Extraordinarily* well. Even men who are making tragic mistakes can course-correct and find success. I've watched men of mediocrity become men of strength and commitment by examining their lives, recognizing the best things, and then giving up lesser pursuits for greater ones. *Man on the Run* endeavors to help men on their quest toward becoming their best selves.

The issues and ideas presented in *Man on the Run* are not unique to men. I have several zealous, energetic women in my life. These women are trying, at least as hard as I am, to determine which priorities and relationships deserve their greatest commitments. Men and women alike wrestle with their consciences, trying to figure out which decisions they will least regret. While I'm primarily addressing men in these pages, my hope is that women will also find encouragement and direction from *Man on the Run*.

With respect to the stories in *Man on the Run,* I've changed many of the contextual details. I'm deeply indebted to the men and women who have trusted me with their personal information. To protect their privacy, I've changed information such as names, occupations, and settings. I did not change any substantive information, and whenever I provided a quote, I attempted to use the exact words from that moment.

Everyone wins when hyper-hobbied men live energetic lives of balance and integrity. *Man on the Run* seeks to provide ideas and strategies that will help us live and finish well. Together. I invite you to keep flipping these pages and join me on this journey.

Great souls are not those who have fewer passions and more virtues than others, but only those who have greater designs.

—FRANÇOIS DE LA ROCHEFOUCAULD

1

MAN OVERBOARD

"**G**reat, because that's exactly what you need . . . *one more pursuit!*"

The playful sarcasm in my wife's voice was thicker than the syrup on my pancakes. It was a blustery, cold day in January. Jagged ice crystals like ornate daggers crept inward from the corners of our windows. My son, Aidan, and I had snuggled under a quilt to eat pancakes and watch a bow-fishing video. The guys on the screen were seated backward as their boat raced down the Mississippi River. Thousands of Asian carp, stimulated by the motor, jumped back and forth in the wake. The shooters launched arrows, one after another, piercing fish mid-jump. To an adrenaline-seeking boy, and his seven-year-old son, this was pretty awesome stuff.

Between our "oohs" and "aahs," I'd shouted to Jamie in the kitchen that Aidan and I were "definitely trying this bow-fishing thing next summer!"

She poked her head into the family room, made her

comment, then playfully reminded me that this would make passion number thirty-four and counting.

I deserve every bit of Jamie's ribbing. As I write this chapter, I'm sitting in our living room, less than a hundred feet from evidence of my thirty-three passions. My garage houses a sixteen-foot aluminum bass boat, an old surfboard, and a closet whose doors won't shut because it's overstuffed with footballs, softballs, and smacked-up golf balls. Our upstairs closet looks like the shoe department in a sporting-goods store, housing river sandals, hunting boots, and several worn-out pairs of running shoes. The back corner of our basement stores my bow and arrows, chest waders, and numerous decoys. In a month or so, this area will likely contain bow-fishing gear.

Something must have happened when I was a kid. At some point, perhaps around the age of two, the Lord must have looked down into my toy box full of rubber balls and action figures and said, "Be fruitful and multiply." Multiply they did. Today, our three-story home, which appeared spacious before we moved in, is cramped and overrun with the fruitful multiplication of Zeke's playthings.

I'm a hyper-hobbied man. Yet I'm passionate about more than just sports. The number of books in my library hints at a book fetish. My Internet history reveals an inordinate amount of time spent researching coffee growers and distributors. Our kitchen cabinets store my end-grain maple cutting board, a couple Santoku knives, and aluminum-core cookware, all evidence of a wannabe chef.

I've lived the first thirty-nine years of my life by Irishman Laurence Sterne's creed: "A large volume of adventures may be grasped within this little span of life, by him who interests his heart in everything."

"Everything" might be a slight overstatement. There are a few pursuits that I haven't thrown myself into. But then, they involve knitting needles, scrapbooks, and shopping malls, so they don't really count anyway, right?

I'm a simple case, really. Like many men, I don't handle inactivity well. My lowest lows—the times when I feel blue or despondent—come to me when I'm sitting on my hands wondering what to do. I keep busy in order to keep sane. On my days off, I fish, exercise, or clean the garage. In the evenings, I write, wrestle with my kids, or play basketball at the fitness center. I even started cooking because it gives me something to do during that restless hour between when I get home from work and when it's time to sit down for dinner.

Some people enjoy large blocks of time with nothing planned. I don't understand those people.

I need more than busy-ness, though. I need to be challenged. An after-dinner stroll around the neighborhood holds little appeal. But I'll walk for hours if there's the chance a pheasant might flush or the next swing might be the golf shot of my life. Likewise, I can't sit for fifteen minutes and do nothing. But I can plant my rear in a tree stand from sunup till sundown, listening for the snap of a twig, the faintest indication that a deer might be walking in my direction. In order to enjoy time, I need something to do, and that something must hold the power to thrill me.

Perhaps this is why I'm always looking to pick up another pursuit—all the more opportunity for adventure. This morning at church, a man asked me if I liked to ice fish. I replied, "You know . . . I bet I *will*. Ask me in a couple of weeks." With that, I went home and researched ice fishing online. Sigh.

My one consolation is that I'm in good company. Not every

man has thirty-four hobbies. Some have twenty-one. Some have eleven. Some have only two or three. It's not about the number. I've known several men who need only one endeavor to consume their lives. Every man is different when it comes to what jump-starts his heart. He's unique, but not alone. He's surrounded by millions of pursuit-driven men scurrying around the offices, lakes, ballparks, and kitchens of our country.

I am not anti-pursuits. In fact, I believe very deeply that the human spirit was designed for challenge, stimulation, and even risk. Men were made to be on the run.

It's hard to be a man today. Our culture's expectations for men are confusing and contradictory. Men are called to lead at home, in the office, and in the community, often simultaneously. They're expected to be rugged and masculine yet gentle and tender. We want men to maintain a solid presence at work, *and* in the home, *and* in society, *and* in the church. Our culture has a thousand ideas about masculinity.

Men sense these fragmented images and expectations, and they feel overwhelmed. But the external messages aren't the only source of tension. Most of the men I've encountered put tremendous pressure on themselves to excel. They want other people's respect. They want to respect themselves. They believe that these two outcomes *only come* when they achieve greatness in all things. Most men I know cut themselves very little slack.

The demands from inside and out, along with the everyday stress of ordinary living, can foster toxic stress levels. I worry about guys who don't have a way to get swept up in the occasional adventure. Men who don't have healthy ways to experience risks, rewards, and challenges tend to find harmful ways.

The movie *Fight Club* perfectly illustrates a man's need for the occasional thrill. Ed Norton's character, the narrator, is an automobile-company employee struggling desperately with boredom and insomnia. He doesn't know how to deal with a life void of risks, rewards, and challenge. He tries faking various terminal diseases so he can attend support groups. There is something about hearing others bare their souls and share their pain that awakens him—for a little while. Joining the support groups helps him sleep and feel alive for a few weeks, but eventually, his boredom and insomnia return. He returns to feeling sterile and dull.

Then the narrator meets Tyler Durden, a soap salesman. One night, outside at a bar, Tyler demands that the narrator hit him in the face. After some coaxing, the narrator does, and the two men have a fistfight in the parking lot. Fists slam into cheekbones. Blood flows. Bruises form. Yet when it's over, they realize that the fight made them feel alive. Tyler and the narrator start up a "Fight Club," giving other bored, under-adventured men a chance to experience the same adrenaline rush. By the end of the movie, fight clubs are operating in every major city, proving that men all around the nation are crying out to feel alive.

Fight Club makes a fascinating social commentary; most men shrivel up and die inside when they're not regularly involved in some form of adventure. The movie apparently struck a nerve with men in America. A "Gentleman's Fight Club" started up in Menlo Park, California, in 2000.[1] In 2006, a young man was injured in a fight club in Arlington, Texas, and the event was recorded and sold on DVD.[2] As unhealthy as they are, these fight clubs illustrate author John Eldredge's point that, "Adventure, with all its requisite danger and wildness, is a deeply spiritual longing written into the soul of man."[3]

Serious problems follow bored men. Men should be combustible goods, regularly ignited and set ablaze by challenging endeavors.

What's more, when men attack their pursuits with over-the-top enthusiasm, they often accomplish wonderful things. Last summer, I returned from an archery hunt in Alaska with excruciating pain in both feet. It felt as if someone was stabbing the padded undersides of my toes with scalpels. My physician, Dr. Buhlke, who was nicknamed "All or None Buhlke" by his medical-school colleagues, spent an entire night pounding cheap coffee and searching medical journals for information on my condition. By his third pot of coffee, as the sun was rising, he correctly diagnosed my injury (Morton's neuroma) and put me on the proper medicine.

Last week, I ran a 5K—pain-free—because "All or None Buhlke" wouldn't rest until he solved my problem. Let us praise pursuit-driven men!

Immeasurable good has come from zealous men launching themselves into their passions. America's independence from Britain is due in part to John Adams's obsessive commitment to the revolution. Michelangelo's eccentric dedication to his craft gave us the "Creation of Adam" painting in the Sistine Chapel. We wouldn't have the songs "Amazing Grace," "Where the Streets Have No Name," or "Crazy Love" if John Newton, Bono, and Van Morrison weren't at least a little over the top as artists. And while I admit that it hardly compares to America's liberty or the most famous painting in Rome, my family has enjoyed some pretty scrumptious meals because I came home from work and "went crazy" in the kitchen with my cutting board, Santoku knife, and aluminum-core pans.

I love to read biographies of great men doing great things. *The Perfect Mile* by Neal Bascomb is just such a book. In this work, Bascomb describes three men's simultaneous race to break the seemingly impossible four-minute-mile barrier. Wes Santee from Kansas, John Landy from Australia, and Roger Bannister from England not only battled the mental and physical challenges laid down by the four-minute mile, but they also battled one another. Whenever one man scheduled a race to attempt to break the mark, the other two waited anxiously by the radio for news on the outcome.

Each man poured himself into this goal, radically adjusting his lifestyle to shave tenths of a second off his four-lap journey around a quarter-mile track. Bascomb records:

> All three runners endured thousands of hours of training to shape their bodies and minds. They ran more miles in a year than many of us walk in a lifetime. They spent a large part of their youth struggling for breath. They trained week after week to the point of collapse, all to shave a second, maybe two, during a race—the time it takes to snap one's fingers and register the sound. There were sleepless nights and training sessions in rain, snow, and scorching heat. There were times when they wanted to go out for a beer or a date yet knew they couldn't. They understood that life was somehow different for them, that idle happiness eluded them. If they weren't training or racing or gathering the

will required for these efforts, they were trying not to think about training and racing at all.[4]

When Roger Bannister ran a mile in 3:59.4 in Oxford on May 6, 1954, he made history. *Forbes* magazine labeled that chilly moment on a damp English track the "greatest athletic achievement" of the past one hundred and fifty years.[5] Bannister broke what many saw as a physically impossible barrier.

He also shattered a psychological hurdle, raising the ceiling and opening the gate for others to follow. Forty-six days after Bannister's moment of glory, Landy made headlines with a time of 3:57.9. By the end of 1957, sixteen runners had followed Bannister's cleat marks into the realm of the subfour elite.

Today, the world record for the mile is 3:43.13. Hicham El Guerrouj from Morocco ran that inconceivable time in 1999 in Rome. I cannot comprehend what it feels like to travel at that speed; I need a good tail wind even to get my truck to go that fast.

Passionate men serve to inspire us. They add vibrancy and excitement to life. Passionate men and their pursuits aren't the problem.

The problem occurs when guys run after their pursuits with such intensity that they neglect other priorities, *higher* priorities. The problem begins when men go overboard.

OVERBOARD

The movie *The Perfect Storm* closes with Mark Wahlberg's character, Bobby Shatford, floating in the middle of the Atlantic Ocean. As the *Andrea Gail*, the fishing boat he was on, sinks to the depths of the sea, the camera slowly pans out and shows the hopelessness of Bobby's situation; he's overboard, in the center of one of the most violent storms in recorded history, with an expression of absolute despair. The water temperature of the Atlantic in the middle of the winter would have been between 25 and 30 degrees. Bobby has only a few minutes of life left before his body completely shuts down, and you can see the desperation on his face as the camera pans out.

I've seen this same desperation on the faces of dozens of men shocked by the storms they've created.

Located in the Midwest, just three miles north of the Platte River, our church is teeming with sportsmen. When our family interviewed at the church on a Sunday morning in 2005, one deer hunter, Beau, pulled me aside in the foyer and whispered, "Zeke, if you come to Central City, I'll hook you up! You'll have a ton of great places to hunt."

Beau kept his promise. But he had competition; about twenty men invited me to hunt with them that first season. In my first six months as a new senior pastor, I was invited to sit in two duck blinds, hunt deer on four farms, and fish on five private ponds. I thought I'd died and gone to heaven. I remember thinking to myself on a frosty morning, while scanning the sky for incoming geese, *Wow, if this is ministry . . . I can do this!*

Every time the phone rang with another invitation from a sportsman, I'd smile a sly smile at Jamie and say, "I'd better accept. I need to get to know the guys in my church."

I did get to know these guys well. I built many strong relationships over the sulfur smell of gunpowder. But alas, at some point, the demands of ministry picked up, and I needed to spend more time at the church and less in the wilderness. Being a pastor in rural Nebraska proved not to be heaven on earth after all.

Over the past five years, several of my hunting buddies have met with me for counseling. Sometimes they brought their wives. Sometimes they came alone. The problem was typically the same: these men had pursued their passions with such narrow-minded fanaticism that they'd thrown themselves overboard into the middle of a perfect storm.

Men are creatures of tremendous pride and self-respect. By the time a man asks to meet me at my office, as opposed to the deer woods, things are in a pretty desperate state. He's caught in the throes of a hurtful addiction, or his life is severely out of whack. The recurrence of this theme has overwhelmed me during my first five years as a pastor.

Men usually know when they've gone too far with a pursuit. You hear it in their language. Whether you watch hunting videos, golf tournaments, or SportsCenter, you'll hear men frequently use the words *obsession* and *addiction* to describe their pursuit. One outdoor-sports company even goes so far as to use the slogan "It's not a passion, it's an obsession."

To be addicted means "to devote or surrender [oneself] to something habitually or obsessively."[6] When someone admits to an addiction or obsession, he's admitting that he's no longer in control. He's no longer driving the bus. The bus is driving him. We laugh about these labels, largely because they resonate with us, but these words—*obsession* and *addiction*—reveal that something is out of balance.

Yet we hear this language all the time. Actor Zac Efron said, "From day one, I got addicted to being onstage and getting the applause and laughter." Journalist Dan Rather commented, "I got addicted. News, particularly daily news, is more addictive than crack cocaine, more addictive than heroin, more addictive than cigarettes." Basketball player and legendary coach Pat Riley made the statement, "To have long-term success as a coach or in any position of leadership, you have to be obsessed in some way."

These are strong statements. Yet many guys can't communicate who they are without using such extreme language.

Sometimes it's not one particular hobby or interest. Many men are simply addicted to being busy or distracted. A woman in our community came in for marriage counseling this past year. Susan was furious. Her face was crimson red when she walked through the door but somehow managed to reach darker and darker shades as she described her husband to me. I learned several new adjectives in the first ten minutes of our time together.

At one point, I stopped Susan mid-adjective and asked her, "Help me understand the core issue. Does your husband have an addiction?"

Her face hit an even darker shade of red. She replied, "YES! He's addicted to the *next thing*, whatever it is!"

I congratulated Susan for finding the perfect words to describe not only her husband but also 75 percent of the men I've worked with as a pastor. I also told her that she'd wandered dangerously close to my backyard with that statement.

RUNNING HARD, STAYING FOCUSED

Passionate, pursuit-driven men can make great husbands, fathers, friends, and colleagues precisely because of their tenacious tendencies. Yet the same qualities can wreck their lives.

Like lumberjacks in a logrolling contest, many men are aggressive, competitive, and fully engaged in the task at hand. Yet they're easily knocked off balance. When this happens, zealous men can destroy relationships, break commitments, and cripple their consciences.

This doesn't need to happen. Men are capable of living with passion and zeal while remaining balanced and faithful to their most important relationships and priorities. They just need to choose the best pursuits and then run after them with intentionality. Run hard, run well, but run after the right things, the right distances. To do this, men must have a clear picture of which relationships and priorities deserve their highest commitments. They need to recognize the activities they should avoid. They require regular infusions of vision and encouragement. They need the help and support of their wives, children, friends, and greater community. If these basics are in place, watch out. Everyone wins when men are on the run.

When I was a child, I'd race into one challenge after another with boyish fearlessness and determination. I'd lower my head, clench my fists, and give it my best shot. I volunteered for the lead role in a play, tried out as pitcher on our baseball team, and (along with 75 percent of teenage boys in America at the time) signed up for karate after watching Ralph Macchio crane-kick Johnny in *The Karate Kid*. My parents watched me take on a thousand challenges with varied success.

Whenever I picked up a new pursuit, worked hard, and did well, my parents would say, "Way to grab that bull by the horns, Zeke!"

This is what we want for men. We want them passionately

and courageously engaged in life. We want them to rise to new heights and feel alive inside. We want them to grab the bull by the horns and live well.

But how to do all of this while maintaining balance in life—that's the challenge of a lifetime.

Unconsidered, merely indulged, ambition becomes a vice; it can turn a man into a machine that knows nothing but how to run. Considered, it can be something else—pathway to the stars, maybe.

—WALLACE STEGNER, *CROSSING TO SAFETY*

2

RUNNING TOWARD, RUNNING FROM

My selfishness was in full bloom. I'd already bow-hunted three times that week. As a husband, father of three young children, and pastor, heading to the woods more than twice in one week is a bit over the top. Yet at three o'clock in the afternoon, for the *fourth time* in five days, I sat twenty-five feet off the ground harnessed to a pin oak.

I wasn't feeling my usual sense of excitement and antic-ipation. I typically spend the first moments of a hunt visual-izing enormous bucks and well-placed shots. But all I could think about that afternoon was how my three kids were about to wake up from their naps to find Dad gone again. I pictured Jamie racing around the house, cleaning up toys, changing di-apers, and throwing together dinner for five. Feelings of guilt, like bony, angry fists, hammered away at my conscience.

I did something that I'd never done before. I climbed down and went home early. As I walked into the house, I met Jamie at the door. She was throwing away a rolled-up diaper, which, judging from the smell, contained a miniature hog-confinement operation. She had a look of shock on her face when she saw me.

I shrugged my shoulders and said, "I blew it. I hunted too many times this week." I threw my hands up in the air and asked her, "Why in the world do I run so hard after things?"

She raised her eyebrows and replied, "That's the million-dollar question, isn't it?"

Men have dozens of different motives and desires fueling their drive to improve their golf game, advance at work, or help their son win the Pinewood Derby. Men run hard, and to suggest that there is just one reason for that would be naïve on my part.

Yet there are several common motives and desires that can serve as a starting point in understanding men's hearts. In my years of counseling men and their families, I've identified several strong inner drives. I've also found many of these motivations lurking behind my own passionate pursuits. When we understand ourselves, we're best prepared to deal with ourselves. If men will peel back the outer layers of their behavior and take a look inside, I believe that most will find themselves in these upcoming pages. I'm also guessing that wives will be able to pick out their husbands in the following descriptions.

RUNNING TOWARD

RESPECT

Workaholics stay late night after night because they want their boss or their coworkers to view them as productive and committed. Hunters, golfers, and yard enthusiasts spend an inordinate amount of time and money to appear competent to other sportsmen, golfers, and neighbors. I've known men who memorize statistics from sports Web sites so that they can be well armed with the perfect bit of trivia when the conversation veers in that direction.

All boys, whether eight years old or eighty, crave respect. The desire to be viewed as an honorable man is as strong in a man's soul as the desire to eat or sleep.

It's ironic how running after respect backfires sometimes. Many men have hoped to earn their wives' respect by energetically chasing some pursuit, only to find that their fanaticism caused them to lose it. A husband once told me during a counseling session, "I spend hours on our yard every week *for her!*" He stretched his arm out and pointed at his wife as if he was picking a criminal out of a lineup. He looked at me and said, "And do I get any respect? Absolutely not!"

This man's wife snapped back, "Are you kidding me? I couldn't care less about the yard. It's just stupid grass! Do you know how many times I've wanted you to drop that Weed Eater, come inside, and act like a father to your kids?"

This husband had poured hours (and hundreds of dollars) into his lawn in an attempt to win his wife's respect. Talk about a fairly major backfire.

FUN

Cyndi Lauper was right, girls *do* wanna have fun. But so do boys, and they'll run hard and fast after some pursuits purely for the sake of enjoyment. A friend of mine, Steve, competes in several off-road races each year. When he drives his truck in the Baja 1000, he plows through boulder fields, mountain passes, and desert streams at speeds up to 120 miles an hour. I rode in his Baja truck once. I almost soiled my khakis when we hit sixty miles an hour on a smooth dirt track. I can't imagine going twice that fast over the rocky terrain of Mexico's famous desert.

I recently asked Steve if he's had any close calls. He said, "The entire race is controlled chaos. One time, I hit several four-foot potholes and flipped end over end. The truck came to rest on its roof, but we finished the race." I asked him if that moment made him rethink racing. He replied, "No way! It happened too fast to think or rethink anything. We just flipped it back over and kept going."

Steve wants to win. He likes to take home the trophy and the prize money. But more than winning, he likes to have fun, and running his truck at speeds that would make most people curl up in the fetal position and pull a blanket over their heads is sheer pleasure for him.

Each man has his own criteria for what constitutes fun. But the longing for it is a powerful motivator.

SELF-VALIDATION

Not only do men need to feel respected by others, but they also have an essential need to feel valid in their own eyes. They want to know that they count for something, that their lives are worthwhile and make a contribution.

Each man has his own criteria for what makes him worthy, shaped by numerous factors, such as how he was raised, what his family valued, who his role models were, and what characteristics and qualities he admired in other people.

One man might need to build his own car from the ground up in order to feel good about himself, because his dad built his first car when he was a young man. Another man might need to earn a doctoral degree in order to gain self-respect, because his friends are all highly educated. A different man will need to run a marathon in less than three hours, because that's how he has defined success in running.

I was reminded of this when I bumped into an old acquaintance in a health-food store. During our high school years, Greg was thin and gangly and teased mercilessly for his lack of coordination. He wore baggy clothes, walked the halls of our school with his head down, and never spoke up in class. That was Greg in 1988.

In 1998, as I was unloading my basket onto the conveyor belt of the checkout line, an enormous man behind the register said, "Hey, Zeke. How've you been?" The voice seemed familiar, but the enormous, bulky frame that it came from appeared completely foreign. "It's me, Greg Cooper, from high school."

The scrawny kid from high school with serious esteem problems was now two hundred and twenty-five pounds of lean, ripped muscle. He was tan, well dressed, and self-assured. He'd also developed quite a grip; I felt bones pop in my fingers when we shook hands. Greg had transformed himself.

We cracked open a couple of sports drinks and sat and talked for a few minutes. I asked him what had compelled him to change so much. He explained that all through school, he hated himself for being such an easy target. In the ten years since graduation, Greg drank protein shakes, spent three hours a day in the gym, and competed in body-building competitions across the country. His last statement was poignant: "At twenty-seven, I finally like myself."

I shook Greg's hand, then walked out of that store feeling immeasurably thankful that I hadn't been one of the kids who had teased Greg in high school.

Men will climb 29,000-foot mountains, bench press 315

pounds, and ascend to the top of the corporate ladder in their quest to accept themselves. But it's been my experience that many men aren't quite as successful as Greg at finding self-acceptance. I've watched several men reach the summit, bench-press six plates, and sit behind the big mahogany desk, only to realize that they still haven't found what they're looking for. Pursuit-driven men will often move on to another pursuit, hoping that the next one will bring that elusive sense of self-worth and value. But, like the last one, it usually seems that the next one fails, too.

CHALLENGE

A couple of years ago, our family rented a house in South Carolina on the beach. Our children woke up before Jamie and me each morning. They'd be sitting by the sliding glass door, staring longingly out at the Atlantic, when we walked out of our bedroom. As soon as Jamie and I each had a mug of coffee in hand, we'd all walk along the slatted wood trail to the edge of the powder-soft beach. When we reached the ocean, Aidan, my wiry, forty-five-pound son, would clench his fists, make guttural man-cub growling noises, and race into the surf. He'd stick out his chest as if to dare the breakers to knock him down. The second-largest ocean in the world, spanning one-fifth of the earth's surface, didn't intimidate or deter him in the slightest. When he'd get knocked down, he'd stand back up, clench his fists, and take on the ocean again.

One night, after the kids were in bed dreaming of digging crabs and riding boogie boards, Jamie and I left them in the care of Grandma and went for a long walk on the beach. I brought up the topic of Aidan's quest to defeat the ocean each morning. Jamie sighed and said, "You know he's got your soul, don't you? You've been daring the breakers in search of challenge ever since I've known you."

I asked her for an example. She reminded me that in two days, I'd be leaving the sandy beaches of South Carolina to fly to the chilly tundra of Alaska to bow-hunt grizzly bears. "Pretty good-sized wave, don't you think?" she said, squeezing my hand.

Men are challenge-seeking missiles. Whether it's throwing the truck into four-wheel drive and hitting the streets after a blizzard, signing up for an endurance race, or staying up all night to get to the next level of a video game, men love to take on challenges.

INTERMITTENT REWARDS

Intermittent rewards (IRs) are the motivating force behind many obsessed, pursuit-driven men. Here's how IRs work. *Intermittent* means occasional or sporadic. An activity that provides intermittent rewards is one that allows the participant to win *every once in a while*. Not every time but sometimes. Not when we're expecting it but at unpredictable intervals. This unknown, uncertain reward hooks men. If a man found success in a pursuit every time he played, the excitement would disappear. If he lost every time he played, he'd eventually give up. But throw a man an *occasional* bone—hold out the possibility of winning *the next time* he plays—and you'll hook him for life.

A fishing guide from Alaska once told me about the men who fly north to angle for enormous trout. He said, "A guy who catches a fish every cast lasts about two hours before he puts his pole down and looks for something else to do. If he catches one fish every twenty minutes, he'll fish hard all week long." That's the allure of intermittent rewards.

Golfers who have felt the thrill of making a hole in one will drop countless dollars on greens fees trying to capture that experience again. Salesmen will hit the streets with passion because they don't know when the next sale might happen. A deer hunter who sees a huge buck in the woods once a season will dream of hunting 365 days a year.

Gambling is a billion-dollar industry, thanks to people's drive toward intermittent rewards. Gamblers will slip coin after coin into the slot, waiting with bated breath for the next jackpot or blackjack. Their sporadic wins cause them to return to the casino again and again with unbridled optimism. Most people lose when they gamble. Casinos never go broke. It doesn't take an advanced degree in statistics to appreciate that people lose more money than they win. Yet gamblers keep coming back because *maybe next time* they will win. This is the alluring and addicting power of intermittent rewards, and it drives many men to succeed the next time. Perhaps.

SENSE OF BELONGING

The Army has the male heart figured out. Its television commercials to recruit young men are brilliant. I'm a middle-aged father of three young children, and I almost called my local recruiter after watching a commercial showing muddy men with grimaces on their faces, crawling side-by-side with buddies, through trenches of mud. What young man wouldn't be attracted to that image?

The strongest pull of these commercials is their promise of belonging. The men running the ropes course and jumping out of helicopters are doing these things *together.* The message? Join the military, and find a sense of brotherhood. You watch our back, and we'll watch yours. It is an irresistible idea for many men.

This message that the military communicates in its commercials is often genuine. Many men do find a sense of belonging in the armed forces, especially during wartime. My friends who have served our country overseas returned with strong feelings of camaraderie toward the men with whom they served. One friend refers to his active duty as the worst *and best* time in his life. "I've never felt closer to a group of guys than during my time in Vietnam," he says.

The military isn't the only place to find a sense of belonging. Some have also found it on a basketball court, in a classroom, as part of a street gang, or at a job site. The desire to belong to a brotherhood of friends is rooted very deep in the hearts of men. When a man believes that excelling in an interest or a career will enhance this sense of belonging, he'll put tremendous effort into that endeavor.

THE DREAM

We all carry a vision of what we think will make us happy. This vision could be called our dream or our desired future. Men often struggle to articulate their dreams, but these dreams are there, and they're highly motivating.

It's important to ask yourself what your life would look like if you were perfectly happy. I've had men answer that question by telling me that they want a house with a white picket fence and three kids playing outside. Other men want to be millionaires, drive Bentleys, and own homes in different parts of the world. Some men want to hike the top ten highest mountains in the world and snap a photo to hang on their wall.

The dreams men chase are always evolving, often because men will reach the goal they believed would make them happy only to find themselves disappointed. One of my friends, Craig, is an avid deer hunter. He's spent hundreds of hours in the fields and forests of Nebraska in the past twenty years pursuing big bucks. Part of his dream involved getting within bow range of a monster of a deer. A couple of years ago, Craig shot one of the largest deer killed in Nebraska that season. When he called me from the field to share his success, he was so ecstatic he was hyperventilating. I felt like a Lamaze partner on the other end of the phone, reminding him to relax and breathe.

I spoke with Craig later that night, just six hours after the first phone call. He told me, "You know, shooting that buck wasn't what I expected. I thought the rush would last longer, more than a few hours. But even by tonight, it doesn't feel like that big of a deal."

Men who make their first million adjust their vision. They rarely sit back and enjoy the spoils of life. Instead, they tend to think, *Perhaps I'll be happy when I make my second.* Men who run a marathon rarely hang their finisher's medal on the wall with a sense of finality. You often find these men signing up for their second marathon with a goal to qualify for Boston or setting the goal to run one in all fifty states. Their picture of what's necessary to find true happiness is a moving target.

Men run toward respect, self-validation, challenge, intermittent rewards, a sense of belonging, and the dream. But we're also motivated by running *away* from things, and these drives are equally powerful and motivating.

RUNNING FROM

SHAME

I met with a man, George, for counseling a few weeks ago. He'd been "working late" several nights a week for the past couple of years. His wife, Sharon, had become suspicious of an affair. She finally gave him an ultimatum: George needed to meet with me and tell me what was going on or find a different place to live.

When George arrived at my office for the first counseling session, I asked why he'd been staying late at work every day. Like his wife, I suspected the worst, so I said, "And please don't lie to me."

George's answer was not what I'd expected. "Pastor, from the time I get home until I leave the next morning, I feel horrible about myself. My kids are out of control. The house is falling apart, windows are broken, and the faucets leak. I don't know how to fix things. The bill collectors call every night. There's no place I feel more like a loser than in my own home. I'd rather stay at work, so I find extra stuff to do around the office to avoid going home."

Men will work long hours, fiddle with tools in the garage, or spend countless hours on the golf course or at the gym in order to avoid feeling like a "loser." They prefer to operate in the realm they're competent in and avoid the places they're not.

LONELINESS

Many men will deny feelings of loneliness. It feels like an admission of weakness. Yet most of the men who ask to spend time with me at the church simply want to talk with a friend.

Men are often derided for not being good communicators, but they have their way of signaling that they need companionship. Walking into the office this morning, I received a text message from a man in our church: "In line at the coffee shop. What do you want to drink?" That cup of coffee lasted ninety minutes.

Later that same day, another man from church dropped by to show me the turkey he'd shot that morning from a ground blind. It was a turkey. I've seen turkeys—they all look the same. His visit wasn't about a bird; it was about connection. We chatted about life for an hour by his tailgate. When I got home from church, another man called and asked if I needed any help fixing stuff. He said, "My wife's out of town, and I'm looking for something to do."

Much of my work as a pastor involves being a friend. Many men feel trapped and isolated. Not geographically but relationally. Where I live in the Midwest, the soil is dark black, and men's fingernails are full of it. It's typical for the hardworking men in our area to spend twelve hours a day outside by themselves working on tractors or fixing fences. These hours provide ample time to put together strong opinions on issues of life and culture. Many of the men I know have more thoughts than they have friends to share them with, and this creates a sense of loneliness.

Clearly, men relate differently from women, but they still need to relate. They need companionship and regular opportunities to share their thoughts and feelings. Often the arenas where men are most comfortable involve work or recreation. Give ten guys a basketball court over the lunch hour, and you'll hear relational dialogue as they lace up their shoes, trot up and down the court, and shower before heading back to work. It might not be "deep" talk, but if you listen closely, between the comments of "give me the ball" and "good game," you'll hear men discussing their relationships and other priorities. If you really listen closely, you might even catch them sharing their feelings. Maybe.

Men's desire to run from loneliness is often what motivates them toward certain sports, hobbies, and careers. This isn't a bad thing; there's nothing weak or wrong about feeling lonely. Adam, the first man, felt alone. As he watched every species of bird, fish, insect, and animal parade before him in pairs, he became painfully aware that he was the only creature who was alone. He felt lonely, and men have shared in this powerful emotion since. Men join duck blinds, play in bands, or jog with running buddies in order to run away from these feelings.

CHAOS

Nobody enjoys chaos. Yet in our culture, men are typically the ones with the greatest opportunity to avoid it—at least, chaos as it's experienced in its primary breeding ground, the home.

I go to work each morning, make a pot of coffee, and then settle in for four hours of studying, counseling, and meetings. All the while, Jamie's at home in the crazy zone, kissing endless boo-boos, cleaning up spills, and breaking up hair pulling and top-of-the-lung screaming matches over who gets the markers and who gets the crayons. My work often feels "heavy," but Jamie deals with a different kind of bedlam altogether, the chaos of bills, spills, and little pills.

I'm not saying it's fair, but many men put crazy hours into work in order to avoid the chaos and commotion of home. Then, after work, it's not uncommon for these same men to spend hours in the garage, on the bass boat, or hitting dimply white balls around well-manicured golf courses in order to continue their escape.

BOREDOM

Boredom kills the souls of men. German writer Johann Wolfgang von Goethe described boredom perfectly when he said, "A man can stand almost anything except a succession of ordinary days." The drive to break up the monotony with something exciting is the motivation compelling many hard-charging men.

In my nine years as a pastor, I've learned that pornography is one of the biggest issues men struggle with. Whether it involves a movie, a magazine, or a Web site, I've watched sexual straying wreck more marriages, careers, and relationships than any other drug or addictive behavior. Pornography use is one of the largest systemic problems in our society.

As I've counseled addicted men, boredom is the most frequent reason they give me for why they view porn. I met with a man a few weeks ago after his wife discovered his interactions with pornography on their home computer. When I asked him what was going through his mind in the moments leading up to his "me time" on the computer, he replied, "I just get so bored. I don't know what to do with myself, so I log on."

Many guys would rather be overworked and exhausted, or stimulated by hurtful things, than aware of the slow passing of time. They'll throw themselves into a pursuit in order to stave off the beast of boredom.

DISAPPOINTING OTHERS

Some men would rather get caught between a mother bear and her cubs than disappoint someone they respect. They'll pour themselves into their work or a hobby out of the fear that if they don't come through, they'll let down their boss, friends, or family.

I have a vivid memory from high school. My best friend, Thom, and I were playing Frisbee in his backyard before going out for the night. His dog, Chause, chased rabbits and squirrels while we played. When we were done tossing the disk around, we flopped down onto the ground, and I threw the Frisbee across the yard and yelled for Chause to "fetch it up!"

Chause bounded off, picked up the Frisbee in his mouth, and brought it back to me. He dropped the disk at my feet, but before I could pat him on the head and praise him, he raced over to Thom. He plopped down onto the grass, wagged his tail, and looked up at Thom with his mahogany brown eyes. Thom scratched his dog between the ears and on the tummy, and then I threw the Frisbee again and yelled for Chause to fetch. We repeated the cycle several times. Each time, Chause returned it to me and then ran over to Thom, his master, for praise.

Like Chause, most men have a few people in particular whom they especially want to please. It might be a man's boss, neighbor, or a friend that he admires. It could be his wife. I'd suspect that nine times out of ten, it's a man's father. But whoever a zealous man's "Thom" is, he'll have unending energy and enthusiasm to run hard in order to please him.

AMALGAM OF MOTIVATIONS

It's often hard for men to pinpoint the reasons they run so hard after a particular interest. Let's examine my motives for bowhunting a fourth time in one week. When I ask myself *why* I felt such a strong pull to the woods, I suspect a variety of motivations. Intermittent rewards are always a factor in my drive to hunt or fish. I'm the classic sportsman. I've been known to say, "Just one more cast," over and over again until one of my fishing buddies has to force me to put my pole away and turn the boat for home. I always expect that the next time on the water or in the woods will be my most successful outing ever. Intermittent rewards certainly compelled me to hunt that day.

But I also needed to escape boredom. That particular afternoon was slow—the kind of day when the phone doesn't ring, nobody drops in to visit, and time seems to move at half-speed. I had to do something to fight off the humdrums, and hunting always provides an adventure.

I also suspect that I was driven by my need to feel respected. Many of my closest friends hunt; they appreciate how hard it is to get within bow range of a deer and then make a good, ethical shot. I enjoy hearing the respect in their voices when I call and report that I punched another tag. I enjoy communicating my respect to them in their moments of success, too. The desire to feel respected was certainly a part of my motivation during that over-the-top week of hunting.

That week, for all of these intertwined reasons, I made a poor decision and took my pursuit a step too far. Like every man, I'm an amalgam of motivations. I confuse myself a good share of the time. I'm certain that many men will feel this way when they examine why they run so hard after their favorite pursuits. Our motivations are matters of the heart, and the heart can be difficult to understand.

But it's not impossible. A man often needs help from his wife and friends, but he *can* discern what makes him chase his passions with dogged intensity. Once he has a grasp on why he runs so hard, he can evaluate whether his drives are healthy. He can ask himself, *Does my energy for a certain passion spring out of a healthy, ordered heart? Or does my passion signal that there is a problem inside?*

The same activity can be healthy for one man and unhealthy for another. One man might be passionate about his work because he experiences a sense of challenge or brotherhood on the job site or feels a deep sense of commitment to provide for his family. Another man might be working just as hard in the same job, but his passion is fueled by shame. Perhaps he's driven by insecurity, feeling that he must overachieve in order to measure up to other people. The same pursuit, two entirely different motivation sets. Once men identify their drives, they can decide if they are satisfied with them or if they need to change or heal something that isn't working.

But the first step is evaluation, figuring out which passions are causing pain.

There is one pain I often feel, which you will never know. It is caused by the absence of you.

—AESCHYLUS

3

WHEN PASSIONS CAUSE PAIN

You can die from drinking too much water. You can die from breathing too much oxygen. You can even die from laughing too much. In 1975, Alex Mitchell, a bricklayer from England, arrived home from work, kicked off his shoes, and turned on his favorite sitcom, *The Goodies*. A skit came on called "Kung Fu Kapers," showing a Scotsman battling chocolate pudding with his bagpipe. Alex laughed for twenty-five minutes until his heart stopped beating.[1]

Good things, *in excess,* become toxic.

A distance runner from Nebraska illustrated this truth for me a few years ago. Dave coached cross-country for a local college and competed in marathons around the country. He was famous for making his team log one-hundred-mile weeks with him. Dave won several national coaching honors for his team's dominance.

It takes more than a touch of fanaticism to log one-hundred-mile weeks on a regular basis. You have to plan your entire schedule around your workouts. When you go to bed, what you eat, even when you work are determined by how far you need to run on any particular day. Dave's monthly budget also orbited around his running. A pair of running shoes costs about $120 and lasts about four hundred miles. Dave purchased a pair a month.

Of all the people and priorities in Dave's life that suffered because of his running, it was his wife, Linda, who sacrificed the most. Dave was always running, sleeping, or at work. On the weekends, he was either at cross-country meets or running in a marathon. He went to bed early, got up early, and wasn't around much between those two events. Linda spent most evenings and weekends alone, wishing for more time with her husband.

After fifteen years of marriage, Linda had had enough. She gave him an ultimatum. One night, when Dave returned home from a twelve-mile tempo run, she said, "It's either your hundred-mile weeks or me. You can't have both anymore."

Dave's running log didn't change. His ring finger made the adjustment.

Running is a good thing. It relieves stress, strengthens the heart, and increases overall energy level. Yet Dave's involvement with running caused him to break his commitments. Fifteen years earlier, as he stood at the altar, he'd promised Linda a deeper level of mutuality and intimacy. He'd promised her that she would be his priority. Dave took a good thing too far, and his passion caused pain.

WHEN GOOD ISN'T GOOD

The idea that necessary and good things can become hurtful isn't easy for zealous men to grasp. People tend to operate in simple categories. They often decide whether something is a positive activity or a negative one. Once they deem an interest good, they tend to give themselves a blank check for involvement. Once a pursuit is determined to be positive, any amount of time and money and energy seems justifiable.

Work is a common example of this simplistic way of categorizing our interests as either positive or negative. It's a necessary and good thing. God created us to work, which makes this activity essential. Even before the fall, Adam and Eve enjoyed tending to the garden.

However, I've watched several men *work* themselves into miserable situations. I spoke with one man several years ago who was having trouble in his fourth marriage. Norm's wife was irritated by his eighty-hour weeks at the office. Norm was a brilliant lawyer who loved his career. But three women had reached the point where they'd had enough, and a fourth appeared to be following close behind. When I asked Norm if he felt that something was out of balance with his career, he was astonished by the question. He replied, "It's my work!" As a young man, fresh out of law school, Norm had put work into the "good" category. From that point on, it was untouchable.

Men can take just about anything too far. I even have a friend who helps people to the point of causing pain. "No" is not in Jay's vocabulary. You'll see his truck parked at different houses around town most nights of the week, while Jay is inside friends' garages or houses, fixing cars, leaky faucets, or broken appliances. Everyone around town thinks Jay is an extremely generous, thoughtful man. His wife doesn't quite see it that way. Sarah is perpetually frustrated. Her husband's willingness to help others costs her time with her husband. Jay consistently puts off important discussions, cancels dates, and "goes missing" several hours a week.

It's not enough for men to determine whether a pursuit is good or bad; they must also choose wisely how far to take their interests.

THE "TOO FAR" LINE

My wife and I love to travel. We went to Ireland together before we had children. We rented a car, drove on the left side of the road, and made our way around the western coastline. One cool, misty afternoon, we pulled into a coastal town for the evening. After a fish-and-chips dinner in the local pub, we asked the bartender how to get to the most scenic, beautiful lookout along the shoreline. He told us to head straight west about a hundred yards, then turn north and walk until we reached the sea. As we were halfway out the door, he yelled, "As you head west, if you hit an electric fence, you'll know you went too far."

Jamie and I left the pub in search of the sea. It was a crisp, dark evening with very little moonlight. We could see the stars and the Milky Way but not the ground in front of us. That didn't slow us down; we trotted across that field without a care in the world.

Until I hit the electric fence. It felt like two slobbering Rottweilers had sunk their teeth into my thighs and were refusing to let go. I was immobilized in pain for about three seconds before leaping backward and falling onto the ground. As I sat there, elbows on my knees, Jamie said helpfully, "Found the fence, huh? Guess we went too far."

Every pursuit has a "too far" boundary, and crossing that line is usually shocking. Where the "too far" boundary is depends on several variables, such as finances, time commitments, stages in life, and other people's expectations.

What is certain is that there is *always* a line to be crossed. Some men notice this line a bit too late. I'll never forget the time I met with Nick, a man from our town who ran into the electric fence.

Nick pulled up to the church that afternoon in a new Lexus coupe, wearing tailored slacks and a crisply starched dress shirt. If not for the desperation on his face, he would have looked like a well-put-together person. When I shut the door and asked him what was wrong, he started sobbing.

"Pastor, my wife just left me after twenty-eight years of marriage."

Like someone buckled into an upside-down car moments after an accident, Nick was in shock. He'd had no idea anything was wrong. For the past twenty-eight years, he'd worked ten hours a day at the office and then another two or three in front of his computer at night trading stocks. His family lived in a large, well-kept, well-furnished home in the country. His children were good students. His wife worked as a part-time secretary at the town library. The first few moments of our time together, Nick kept repeating the statement, "This can't be true. It just can't be true."

As Nick and I talked about his life, it became clear that his favorite pursuit was making a profit and watching his investment accounts grow. There was always time to trade stocks or wine and dine clients. There was never quite enough time to spend time with his wife. For two and a half decades, he crossed the line over and over again.

Nick described how, early in their marriage, Cheryl would get mad at him. She wanted more time with him. She wanted their children to get more time with their dad. Cheryl was a soft-spoken person, but she did her best to communicate her hurt feelings and her expectations for the marriage. Nick admitted to me that he didn't really listen. He also didn't make any changes; he kept working long hours, while promising to free up time in the near future. As Nick and I discussed his marriage, it became clear that Cheryl had slowly given up on her husband.

Sometime, about ten years before my meeting with Nick, Cheryl stopped getting mad. Like many men, Nick took his wife's silence as a sign that everything was fine. He had assumed that somehow, perhaps miraculously, things must have improved. This is one of the worst conclusions a man can reach. As a counselor, I'm encouraged by mad, vocal spouses. Anger and passion reveal that there is still life in the marriage. It's been my experience that when there is fight left in a person, there is love. There are expectations and hopes. It's the apathetic spouse who causes me to worry.

This is what happened to Cheryl. She wrote Nick a note, packed up her things, and was out of the house by the time he came home for lunch. When Nick walked through the front door, the house felt eerily vacant. A lamp, a chair, and several books were missing from the living room. The dishes were gone from the kitchen. Empty spaces filled the walls where pictures had hung. A handwritten note on a sticky pad sat atop a stack of divorce papers in the kitchen. It said, "Please fill out. I'll pick them up tomorrow."

Nick told me that he'd do anything to get his wife back. He pleaded with me to call Cheryl and tell her that he was sorry and ask her to give him a second chance.

He was in such a panic that I agreed to make that call. However, calls like that never go well. When I reached Cheryl at her friend's house that evening, there was no emotion in her voice. She said, "I thought Nick might try something like this. No offense, Pastor, but he's had his second chance. Thousands of them. I'm done."

Cheryl meant it. That day with Nick took place almost

five years ago, and he's still living alone. He lost his job a few months after his divorce because of a bout of depression. He still feels that pain in his chest.

I wish I could say that helping a man such as Nick through a disaster like that has been a rare activity. But I've gone through this so many times with men that I've recognized patterns and common themes.

NOT PAYING ATTENTION

The first theme is that when men go too far with a pursuit, they often fail to recognize how deeply they are hurting those around them. Men who cross the "too far" boundary and then experience the consequences of failed relationships often feel shocked. I've had several men say to me, "I had no idea things were this bad!" Some husbands have asked, "Why didn't she say something to me sooner?"

NOT LISTENING

This leads to the second theme. She *did* say something sooner. Most wives, children, friends, and bosses tell men when they cross lines. Hardheaded, hard-charging men just have a hard time *hearing* it. I've been known to race after a pursuit until the people closest to me are at the ends of their ropes. When someone cries or yells, then I'll likely see the lines I'm crossing. But, embarrassingly, it often takes a bullhorn for a comment to register.

I've had to ask my wife to forgive me dozens of times for overstepping lines. I've also asked her more than once, "If things were bothering you so much, why didn't you tell me sooner?" After a well-deserved eye roll, Jamie's usually able to list out for me the numerous times she *did* tell me her feelings.

I'm not alone in this inability to hear others. Forward-moving, energetic men aren't known for being sensitive, acute listeners. They run out the door for work, race from one thing to another, and measure the success of their day by the work they've produced. The softer voices of their spouses and children often blur into the background.

Until someone makes a big statement, like Cheryl made to Nick.

DESPERATION TIME

This leads to the third theme. Men who consistently cross the "too far" boundary typically end up desperate. When things blow up and relationships fall apart, men experience severe emotional pain. I've had guys call me at ten o'clock at night to ask for help. I've had men break down in tears in the hardware store. I even had a man offer me $10,000 if I could fix his marriage. I thought he was kidding, but the look on his face let me know that he was dead serious.

TOO LITTLE, TOO LATE

The fourth and final theme is perhaps the saddest. By the time a man cries in the hardware store, it's usually too late. In all my years of working with desperate men and the people they've hurt, I've only been able to persuade one wife to work things out with her husband and take him back. *One.* I wish it wasn't true. I wish reality wasn't so harsh and I could boast of a much higher success rate of helping desperate men win back what they've lost. But it is what it is. At some point, people who have been continually hurt or neglected give up. Like Cheryl, they stop giving second chances.

I imagine that many men who read about Nick's story will

think, *That will never happen to me. I'll never get swept away with my work or hobbies to that extent.* This may be true. Nick is certainly an extreme example. Many men will cross lines but not experience such a degree of pain and loss.

But the ambitious man's goal shouldn't be simply to avoid disaster, despair, and divorce. That would be a sad, smallish goal. Instead, the goal ought to be to live full, vibrant lives, as Thoreau said in *Walden*, "to live deep and suck out all the marrow of life." Most of the men I know don't just want to settle for decent marriages and mediocre relationships with their children; they want to run after their most important relationships and priorities with energy. They want to live well. *Tremendously* well. That's the high bar we should set.

To live tremendously well requires more than just balance; it requires that men examine the deepest parts of their lives to identify the things that might be broken.

The heart of a man is a complex system. If the mind is the place of thoughts and feelings, then the heart is the place where a man assesses the options and then chooses his actions. The heart is where character is established. If the heart is healthy, the man is healthy. If the heart is broken, the man is broken. If a man will examine his heart and ask himself why he crosses lines and hurts others, he'll likely gain a glimpse of what isn't working. He'll find thoughts and feelings and choices that aren't helping him accomplish his deepest goals.

I first took a look inside my heart about twenty years ago, when I was nineteen years old. It wasn't an easy process or a fun stage of life for me, yet it led to a life that I had no idea was possible. The next chapter tells my story.

**Everyone I know goes away in the end,
you could have it all, my empire of dirt.**

—JOHNNY CASH, "HURT"

**Happy are the poor in spirit, for theirs
is the kingdom of heaven.**

—JESUS

4

BROKEN OUT OF THE BOX

Aidan, my six-year-old son, had just opened his final Christmas present, a metal detector. He'd been pining for one ever since I'd planted the idea in his mind a month earlier when we'd gone turkey hunting in the woods along the Platte River.

At sunset that day, a flock of thirty birds tramped through two-foot drifts of powdery snow seventy yards from our ground blind. Seventy yards is a long shot with archery gear. But this was the last hunt of the season, and Aidan begged me to take it.

My first arrow missed by about two feet but made the lead turkey hop and pick up its speed. My second shot missed by so much that the birds didn't notice. We watched the flock wander off into the timber before slipping from the blind to search for my arrows.

Finding two arrows in a snowdrift is about as easy as shooting a turkey at seventy yards. Aidan's red mittens pawed at the snow for about ten minutes before he said, "I don't think we're going to find them, Dad."

I replied, "You know, Bubba, if you had a *metal detector*, you could find those arrows for me."

The stage was set. For the next month, all I heard about was metal detectors and rescuing arrows. On Christmas morning, when he ripped off that first piece of wrapping paper, revealing the picture on the box, he squealed, "Dad, now I can find your arrows!"

His hot little hands opened the package of batteries while I unscrewed the back panel. I snapped in six AA batteries and tightened things back up. Lights flashed on. Time to try it out. We threw a nickel on the floor and waved the sensor over it. Nothing. I dialed up the sensitivity. Still nothing. Aidan had a concerned look on his face as I flipped through the ridiculously thick instruction manual. We fiddled with that lifeless device for thirty minutes, to no avail. It was a dud, broken out of the box.

I'll never forget the image of my son sitting cross-legged on the floor in the glow of the Christmas tree lights, holding that metal detector as if it was the family pet that had just died in his arms.

That's how it is in life; things arrive broken out of the box. "Check engine" lights flash on as you drive off the lot. Lights flicker in the house you've just built. Buttons fall off during the first washing. It begins with a Christmas present when you're six years old, but by the time you're forty, a thousand things have let you down.

We can survive damaged *things*. We can fix them, replace them, or simply move on. Stuff is just stuff. What's harder to live with is the brokenness we see in ourselves.

We all enter this life broken out of the box. We squeeze

from the womb as adorable, fleshy balls of mixed motives and selfishness. We scream when we're hungry. We grab what we want and throw the things we don't. We begin life utterly focused on ourselves.

Babies can get by with mixed motives and selfishness. Their sparkling eyes and pudgy little thighs cover over a multitude of issues. I know this firsthand as a dad. The sun rose and set in my three children's faces. They could have thrown my steak into the toilet, but if they smiled at me while they flushed, I would have lassoed the moon for them. Selfishness almost seems cute at times—in babies.

It's not so cute in a teenage boy. People don't just grow up and out of their brokenness, and sometime during my high school years, I started to feel disgusted by what I saw inside myself. I imagine that to many of my friends and family, I looked relatively put together. I had lots of friends and was part of a swim team that won state three out of my four high school years.

As I examined my life, I realized that my drives and motivations were all messed up. I wanted to be popular, not because of a deep love for people, but because I wanted to prove to myself that I was likable. In college, I wanted to make good grades and go to physical therapy school, not primarily to help others heal and recover but because I wanted to make money and achieve a certain lifestyle. I had a strong desire to be the best swimmer, pitcher, and three-point shooter, not so that my team would win but so that I could experience personal glory. Many of my behaviors and the products of my life—popularity, decent grades, and state championship medals—were driven by unhealthy motivations.

Even though I was good at managing impressions and looking good to others, I didn't look good to myself. I had very little self-respect, and this pained me.

A MILLION MICE

If we can't avoid pain, we try to distract ourselves from it. As a man who continually cracks his head on the ceiling as he walks down the stairs learns to duck, I learned to duck, to stop looking inside. Like many men, I ducked by filling up my life with distractions. When I went off to college, I made sure that every free moment was spent with a hobby, a sport, a job, or any activity that would keep me from slow, reflective moments.

Peter Kreeft described my first year and a half in college with eerie precision in his book *Christianity for Modern Pagans*:

> We *want* to complexify our lives. We don't have to, we *want* to. We want to be harried and hassled and busy. Unconsciously, we want the very things we complain about. For if we had leisure, we would look at ourselves and listen to our hearts and see the great gaping hole in our hearts and be terrified, because that hole is so big that nothing but God can fill it.
>
> So we run around like conscientious little bugs, scared rabbits, dancing attendance on our machines, our slaves, and making them our masters. We think we want peace and silence and freedom and leisure, but deep down we know that this would be unendurable

to us, like a dark and empty room without distractions where we would be forced to confront ourselves. . . .

If you are typically modern, your life is like a mansion with a terrifying hole right in the middle of the living-room floor. So you paper over the hole with a very busy wallpaper pattern to distract yourself. You find a rhinoceros in the middle of your house. The rhinoceros is wretchedness and death. How in the world can you hide a rhinoceros? Easy: cover it with a million mice. Multiple diversions.[1]

Something was missing in my life. I couldn't find it, so I played intramural volleyball, basketball, and Frisbee golf. I lifted weights five nights a week, tried out for the baseball team, and played city rec softball. I took a full load of classes, hunted most weekends during the winter, and fished most weekends in the spring. I surrounded myself with people, partying several nights a week. If a slow moment crept up and surprised me, I'd pop in on a friend or run over to the fitness center. *Squeak, squeak.*

I'll never forget one of the nights that the million mice scattered and I had to take a hard look at the rhinoceros in my house. I'd gone to a fraternity party with friends. I should have felt great that night, optimistic. Finals were a few weeks away, and I was heading into them with a 3.5 GPA. My four-on-four basketball team had just won the intramural tournament that afternoon. I'd just signed a contract to lifeguard at the largest outdoor pool in Nebraska. From the outside, things looked pretty good. There wasn't a crisis, a damaged relationship, or a stressful situation to be found.

Yet all I wanted to do that night was escape. As I left my dorm room and walked across the street to the party, I wanted to flee from my thoughts and feelings by drinking as much beer as possible. As I entered the fraternity, I had my plastic cup in my hand and a mission to accomplish. By ten o'clock, I was sitting on a ratty paisley couch in the basement of the fraternity, waves of nausea rolling over me. A friend walked by at about 10:30, saw my pasty white face, and helped me stumble across the street and back to my dorm room.

I'd gone through two roommates that year—one flunked out, and the other transferred schools—so I had a double-occupancy room to myself. My friend unlocked the door and helped me lie down on the bed. I couldn't sleep, though. The large volume of alcohol coursing through my veins made me sit up and gasp for air every time I tried to shut my eyes. I got out of bed and sat cross-legged on the cold, tiled dorm-room floor until five o'clock the next morning.

The rhino sat beside me the entire time. For about six hours, I vacillated between feelings of self-hatred and feelings of helplessness. I was so tired of myself. I also felt a strong sense of panic. I had no idea how to change my life.

Sometime around midnight, I picked myself up off the floor, walked to my bookshelf, and pulled down the hardback Bible that a Gideon had placed in my room before I'd moved in. I'm still amused by the strangeness of that act. I'd never held a Bible in my hands before. I'd never thought deeply about spiritual things. I'd only been to church twice in my life, and I felt out of place both times. Yet, for some reason, in that lonely moment, I picked up the Bible. Picking it up was about all I could do with it. I was too intoxicated to read. I got as far as Genesis 1:6 before setting it down on the floor beside me.

What an odd moment. I suppose that by reaching out to the Bible that night, I was demonstrating to myself that my way of thinking for the first nineteen years of my life hadn't worked. Those lonely hours sitting on the floor symbolize the moment when I became desperate enough to face my rhino and look for help. Nothing drastic happened that night. I finally fell asleep about the time the rest of the dorm was waking up for breakfast.

I limped through the rest of my freshman year of college, lifeguarded over the summer, and returned to Wesleyan in the fall. But there was something different about me when I hit campus for my sophomore year. I had a new craving for answers—answers to more than just the questions raised in classes. I wanted to explore philosophy and religion. I wanted to find truth. I'd regularly set up appointments with professors to ask them for their opinions on life and their fields of expertise. I asked my biology professors about their beliefs on the origins of life. I asked my psychology professors for their thoughts on relationships and self-esteem. I asked my philosophy professors for their opinions on agnosticism, atheism, and various forms of theism. I was in a small school with accessible professors—the perfect setting for serious exploration.

I couldn't find a Christian professor at Nebraska Wesleyan University. Best that I could tell, the number of Christians at my liberal-arts college could have *almost* filled the roster of an eight-man football team. Yet I found and befriended one of them, a guy named Matt. He was a biology student, so we attended the same classes. We ate dinner together most evenings. We lifted weights, hunted, and hung out on the weekends. Matt was a relatively new Christian. He'd put his faith in Jesus during his senior year in high school, as his dad was dying of cancer.

Matt's faith was mysterious, fresh, and attractive to me. His approach to discussing spiritual things fit me well. He never pushed or pounded the Bible at me. He figured that when I had a question, I'd ask. And I did, several times a week. Matt responded to my questions in the same way each time. It didn't matter whether we were shooting hoops in the gym or eating breakfast at the cafeteria, whenever I asked him about his faith, he'd pull his Bible from his backpack, flip to a passage, and then hand it to me, asking, "What's this say?"

In all of my exploring that fall, it was Matt's dog-eared study Bible that made the most sense to me. The Bible described life and my situation with striking accuracy. Verses such as Romans 7:18 described my suspicions perfectly: "For I know that nothing good dwells in me, that is, in my flesh. For I have the desire to do what is right, but not the ability to carry it out." Everything inside me resonated with that verse. I wanted to do what was right. I wanted to be a good man. I just couldn't find the power to transform myself. This flip-flopping between who I was and who I wanted to be was exhausting.

I also had a sense that if there was a God, He must be pretty disappointed in me. Romans 3:23 confirmed this: "For all have sinned and fall short of the glory of God." I didn't need convincing that there was such a thing as sin or that I'd participated in it. By the time I read Romans 3:23, everything inside me suspected that there was a God. What's more, if there was a God, I knew He must be perfect. And if He was perfect, and He created me, He must have expectations for how I should live. And if He had expectations, I'd certainly fallen short of them. I hadn't measured up to *my* hopes and expectations for myself; there's no way that I'd lived up to His.

Bible verses such as Romans 7:18 and 3:23 might offend

some people, but they summoned a very different response from me. They gave me a sense of hope, hope that if the Bible contained such accurate statements, then perhaps the entire picture of life described within its pages was true. And if the Bible's picture of life was true, then there was a purpose to life. There was a Creator. And, as I'd soon learn in the New Testament, there was a way to deal with being broken out of the box.

Throughout my sophomore year, I was in hot pursuit of God. Everything else took a backseat. Each night, I'd lie in my loft, next to the large picture window overlooking the court-yard, and I'd work my way through a few chapters in the New Testament. For six weeks, I cut out the distractions; I studied less, put off friends, and burned out several light bulbs in my reading light. When I think back to those evenings reading through my Bible in my loft, it's a warm memory, like putting on a sweatshirt just out of the dryer. The Gospel came alive in me with every thin, French-milled page I turned.

I didn't tell anyone about my new pursuit. Not right away, at least. I just kept flipping pages. I wanted to make sure that I was forming an accurate picture of the God I was getting to know. I'd never met someone quite like Him before. He seemed almost too good to be true. He's perfect, without sin, yet He loves sinners. He pursues people who are broken out of the box with a strong, wild, undeterred love. He never turns away from a broken man who cries out for help. Nobody is too broken, too messed up, for God. The more I read, the more I felt drawn to this mysterious being.

Two things happened on Tuesday, November 6, 1990. I decided that God was entirely good and that He offered me a different kind of life. I also decided that I was tired of being in control of my life. I'd journeyed to the end of myself and didn't have the legs to go farther.

I told my friend Matt about these two resolutions, and then I asked him if he would pray with me. In his dorm room, I knelt down on the floor, leaned over the residence-hall mattress, and talked to God. The best that I can remember, it was the first time in my life that I prayed. It was a choppy prayer. My words were raw and unpolished. I probably swore; few of my sentences those days didn't involve expletives. I certainly didn't finish with "Amen."

It's probably the best prayer I've prayed. I had one strong desire in that moment: to be close to Jesus, to feel right with Him, accepted by Him. I confessed every sin I could think of. I thanked Him over and over for being patient with me. I told Him that I wanted Him to take over. I asked Him to help me examine my life—my motivations, commitments, and relationships—and show me what needed changing. Then I asked Him to change me.

I've never moved beyond that first prayer. I still ask God to change me every day.

If there's one thing that's painfully clear to me by now, it's that becoming a Christian doesn't instantaneously fix everything in our lives. Wonderful things happen when people trust in Jesus for salvation—they are restored to their Creator, they receive the Holy Spirit, and they become a child of God. When I finished that first prayer, I knew my life had been reoriented. Significant things happen in our moment of faith, but instant perfection isn't one of them.

I sin every day. Like all men, I'm a work in progress. Sometimes the progress is frustratingly slow. Yet I want to live well. I want to grow and change and become a better man. This is where grace comes in. Men who love God still act selfishly and hurt others at times. They take pursuits too far and have to ask for forgiveness. Believing in Jesus doesn't once and for all fix what is broken. It places us in a relationship with the God who cheers men on as they learn to recognize the best things.

Even men like you and me, who were broken out of the box.

You gotta win to get love. I mean, that's just life.

—RICKY BOBBY, *TALLADEGA NIGHTS*

**All the way my Savior leads me, cheers
each winding path I tread.**

—FANNY CROSBY,
"ALL THE WAY MY SAVIOR LEADS ME"

5

THE CHEERING VOICE

THE SCREAMER

My swim coach had anger issues. He would walk up and down the pool, veins popping out of both temples, yelling at his swimmers. Occasionally, he'd lose himself to his anger and jump into the pool fully clothed. He'd stand by the wall, hands cupped over his mouth, and scream into our ears as we did flip turns.

A part of me didn't take it personally. He shouted at boys and girls, grade-schoolers and high-schoolers, good swimmers and bad ones. I'd heard him roar a hundred times, so I knew he was an equal-opportunity screamer. This was just his way.

But a part of me did take it personally. A part of me believed some of what he yelled. When he called me lazy, I felt lazy. When he told me I was an embarrassment, I felt embarrassed. When he told me I wouldn't amount to anything, I lowered my expectations. His yelling convinced me that I was a person who deserved to be yelled at.

My coach's voice affected my motivation to swim. I never wanted to go to practice. When I went to practice and heard his voice, my drive to excel diminished. Much the way a man feels lethargic after eating a cholesterol-laden cheeseburger, I could feel my body getting more and more sluggish with each scream.

After I touched the wall and finished the state swim meet my senior year in high school, I quit swimming. I boxed up my swim caps and goggles, turned down a couple of offers to swim in college, and haven't swum laps for fun or exercise in more than twenty years.

The goal of this book is to cheer men on as they run after their best pursuits. Everyone wins when men chase their key relationships and commitments with energy and enthusiasm. But this is a hard world, nauseatingly hard at times. We make mistakes. We cross lines. We do stupid, selfish things that hurt others and ourselves in painful ways. As we discussed in the last chapter, even men who love God sometimes fall flat on their faces. When this happens, there are usually several voices that are quick to scream our failures at us. The loudest voices, perhaps, are the ones in our own heads.

Men who listen to screaming voices of shame and guilt will not run with their *best* energy. Negative motivations such as shame, guilt, and anger can move men to action. My swim coach knew that I'd swim lap after lap if he kept yelling at me. Some of the swimmers who received his screams ended up at the Olympic trials. He knew that negative motivation was still motivation.

What he didn't know is that I would have swum twice as hard for him had he cheered me on. A few "attaboys," and I would have swum the Atlantic Ocean for him.

Men want to measure up. They want to know that they are

being cheered on. They run their best races when they know that they are deeply loved and perfectly accepted. This cheering voice is given to us as a gift. We hear it only by grace.

THE ONGOING FREE GIFT

Grace is a free gift. We receive grace when we receive something we haven't earned. A few weeks ago, I went to an archery shoot in Utah. A few outdoor writers and professional target shooters were invited to tour the plant of a well-known arrow manufacturer. In the morning, we met the owner of the company and watched a demonstration of how carbon arrows are built.

To spice the event up, the company held a 3-D archery tournament in the afternoon in the mountains outside Orem. They divided up the employees, outdoor writers, and professional shooters into four teams of four people each. The teams were given instructions to shoot at twenty targets, and the top three scores would count. The owner of the company put up a thousand dollars as a prize for the team that finished first.

As an outdoor writer, I hadn't been invited to the plant because of my shooting ability. I'm considerably more accurate with a keyboard than I am with arrows. Shooting side-by-side with some of the best tournament shooters in the world, I had low hopes of impressing anyone.

I'm certain I didn't. In that best-three-arrows competition, my score counted twice out of twenty targets. I was simply outmatched by the majority of shooters that afternoon.

Yet I went home with a share of the prize money. Our team won the tournament, largely thanks to Levi Morgan, the national 3-D Circuit leader at that time. He carried our team. Every shot was intentional; he'd hold his bow perfectly still, control his breathing, and then steadily squeeze off a perfect shot time and again. Levi's shooting was a thing of beauty to watch. My shooting was, well, not quite so beautiful. For two hours, as Levi methodically slipped his arrows into the center rings, I broke mine on branches or searched for them in the forest.

We won because of Levi. However, when our team turned in the score card, I was treated like a champion. People high-fived me. I won a fourth of the prize money.

That was grace, an undeserved gift.

Grace is a word that is frequently used by Christians. Typically, it's used to explain how a person is saved. Many Christians understand that they need grace to be saved. What is not clearly understood is that they also need grace every moment following salvation. It's been my experience that many people, once they place their faith in Jesus, go back to living by performance. Sure, they know they're saved by grace. But once saved, they go back to trying to feel worthy, or valuable, by what they do.

A LOST SIGNIFICANCE

There is something old and deep in the hearts of men that drives them to find significance in what they do. This desire to find self-worth through performance can be traced all the way back to Genesis 3.

In Genesis 2, we find two people who know they are significant. Adam and Eve are perfectly contented. They long for nothing. They've been given life in healthy, strong bodies.

They've been given companionship and sexual excitement. They've been given habitation in the most breathtaking environment this world has ever known.

But with all of these gifts, Adam and Eve's sense of significance and contentment came from their rootedness in God. Distinct from the rest of creation, Adam and Eve had been created in the image of God. Trees, lions, and orchids didn't bear God's image. Only Adam and Eve carried this fingerprint of the divine, as Genesis 1:27 records: "So God created man in his own image, in the image of God he created him; male and female he created them."

Because Adam and Eve had been made in the image of God, they enjoyed an intimate, mutual relationship with their Creator. God walked with them in the garden, and Adam and Eve enjoyed His presence. Like a child snuggled up in a blanket on her father's lap, Adam and Eve felt secure, delighted, and utterly satisfied in God's presence. No shame. No fear. No sense of inadequacy or insignificance. Just pure, complete contentment.

Genesis 2:25 paints this picture of perfect significance and contentment: "And the man and his wife were both naked and were not ashamed." This is a description of more than physical nakedness that led to great sex. Adam and Eve stood fully exposed, vulnerable, before God and each other. Nothing covered their bodies or their minds or their hearts. Who they were was open for all to see, and it felt good and right.

How does Satan persuade two perfectly secure and satisfied people to disobey God?

He convinces them that there is still more to be had.

Satan lied and told Adam and Eve that God was holding something back from them. He told them that there was a pleasure that God didn't want them to enjoy. Eve began to doubt God. Then she ate. Then Adam followed. Then all hell broke loose.

As soon as this satisfied, contented couple disobeyed God, "the eyes of both were opened, and they knew that they were naked" (Genesis 3:7). Before sin, Adam and Eve were fully exposed but felt safe and secure. They had nothing to hide and nothing to prove. When sin came, they noticed their nakedness and felt insecure. This first couple sewed fig leaves to try to cover their nakedness. They hid from God in the bushes. They began to fear the one who had once made them feel perfectly safe. In Genesis 3, Adam and Eve lost the significance they once had in God.

Where do people turn when they do not have significance from being rooted in God?

They turn to themselves. They turn to their performance. Life after Genesis 3 is a life of seeking value and significance in *doing*. If you don't feel good about yourself, try harder. If you don't like yourself or feel that you measure up, work longer. If you struggle with feeling worthy of other people's love and acceptance, strive to overachieve. If you worry about how others look at you, buy more items of status.

The elusive desire that many zealous men run after as they strive to excel at work or in play is that Genesis 2 sense of being naked and unashamed. All people want to feel perfectly accepted by God, other people, and themselves. It's a longing as old as time. Trying to satisfy the longing to feel significance and satisfaction through our performance is like trying to put out a fire by throwing gasoline on it. It only feeds the problem.

PERFORMANCE: THE EXHAUSTING STORY

Men who seek their meaning and significance in the things they do are continually trying to put points on the board. Rewards, prizes, and status symbols are not just things to display on the shelf, they're trophies of significance. Degrees on the wall or trophies on the mantel become symbols men can gaze at to help them feel that their lives have merit and meaning. This is the Performance Story, and many men find themselves in the pages of this tiring book.

The Performance Story reads almost like a formula. Just as four plus four equals eight, people get out of life what they put into it. They reap what they sow. They are valid because of what they produce. Men who live by the Performance Story evaluate their self-worth based on how well they're performing at work, in the home, or with other relationships and hobbies—and they judge others based on performance, too.

This view of life typically leads to formulaic, simplistic conclusions. If people appear to be doing well in life—perhaps making a good paycheck or owning large homes or nice cars—they must *deserve* those results. Likewise, if people are going through hardship, loss, and suffering, it's assumed that if they'd just made better choices or worked harder, they wouldn't be in the messes they're in. At the core of the Performance Story is the belief that people get what they deserve. If someone is getting good things, pat him on the back. If he's getting bad things, shake your head and move on.

It's been my observation that many boys first encounter the Performance Story in their dads, perhaps on a T-ball diamond, at a Pinewood Derby, or after a parent-teacher conference. When a child wins or performs well, he merits his dad's pleasure. He sees pride and acceptance in his father's eyes. When the child doesn't do well, he sees disappointment.

There are few things that sons long for more than their father's pride and acceptance. As soon as they realize that they *earn* these responses from their dad, they set their compass and get to work.

It doesn't take long for this performance pattern to establish. As with deer walking the same path day after day, year after year, deep and often permanent ruts are created in the hearts of boys whose dads expressed their love and acceptance only when their sons performed well.

Boys introduced to the Performance Story when they're young grow up into men who believe they're worth something *only when* they do good things. All across our country, men in their twenties, fifties, and eighties finish each day exhausted from trying to do enough in order to feel valid.

The comedy *Talladega Nights* uses humor to illustrate this toxic idea. Will Ferrell's character, Ricky Bobby, is a down-on-his-luck race-car driver. He lost all self-respect when he started losing races. One night, after he berates himself for losing a video game, his girlfriend says, "You always have to prove yourself. Why?"

Ricky Bobby gives a funny but poignant reply: "You gotta win to get love. I mean, that's just life. Look at Don Shula, legendary coach, look at, uh, look at that Asian guy who holds the world record for eating all those hot dogs in a row, look at Rue McClanahan . . . from the *Golden Girls*, all three people, all great champions, all loved."

"You gotta win to get love." That's the lie that's tucked painfully into the hearts of millions of young and old boys.

That's also the lie that causes boys to clench their fists, pull up their boots, and do everything they can to perform well. Performance must be measured, and it seems in our society, it's judged by who makes the most money, owns the nicest homes, carries the prestigious titles, and earns the advanced degrees. Men will knock themselves out trying to win in order to get love.

If the Performance Story is such an exhausting way to live, why do so many people perpetuate it? For all the hurt this way of life produces, it's an oddly attractive option. People like rules, boundaries, and standards. They like to categorize and compare. The Performance Story provides men with familiar and objective criteria by which they can evaluate others and themselves. The men who can hit the home runs, lead the board meetings, and get elected to office deserve respect. They're the leaders, the heroes, the admirable ones. Those who can't achieve such levels of greatness aren't quite as worthy. As tragic as it is, there's something comforting in being able to categorize people based on performance.

But just because something is comfortable or familiar doesn't make it healthy. People don't always choose what is best for them. As Frederick Buechner said, "Lust is the craving for salt of a person dying of thirst."[1] If men choose to live by the salty Performance Story, they must be willing to die by it. And this way of life slays everyone.

Nobody can overachieve every moment of every day. Eventually, we mess up. When a man bases his sense of self-worth on his performance and then he does something poorly, he feels worthless. I grew up in the Performance Story, and I remember dozens of nights in high school, lying in bed feeling like a failure because I'd placed second at a swim meet or earned a C on a test or I struck out three times in a baseball game.

Getting second, making a bad grade, and striking out don't make anyone a failure. That's an irrational conclusion. Yet when the idea that you're worth something *only when you do well* has been rutted into your mind since childhood, a single failure can make you question your entire existence.

The Performance Story has produced a world full of exhausted men who are trying to prove that they measure up by what they do. This way of life deepens the ache in men's hearts to feel significant, to feel naked and unashamed, to hear someone say, "You are good enough. You do measure up. You are fully accepted."

It doesn't matter whether a man is in a good moment or a bad one. There's no lasting contentment in the Performance Story. There's no joy. Just exhaustion, pressure, and a continual awareness that his self-worth is on shaky ground. Living by performance may be the popular option for men, but it's certainly not the life-giving one.

Life can only be found in living by grace.

REDISCOVERING SIGNIFICANCE

As I discussed earlier in this chapter, it's possible to be saved by grace but then return to living by performance. It's easy to recognize people who are doing this, because they typically feel distant from God. God isn't safe. He's not a loving father who is perpetually pleased with His children. He's judgmental. He's condemning. He's consistently displeased. God, to a performance-driven Christian, is someone to hide from. Like a dog that's constantly scolded, beaten, and made to feel shame, he tucks his tail and hides in the shadows from his maker.

A person who truly understands grace, not just as an idea but also as an identity-shaping force, will want to be with God. We want to be with those who love and accept us. It's in our nature. When we feel worthy and valued and respected by someone, we run toward that person the way a child runs to his dad. We're drawn to people who understand and accept us.

When a man lives by grace, he hears the voice of God telling him, in his good moments and his bad ones, that he's fully accepted. As the old hymn "All the Way My Savior Leads Me" celebrates, when a man lives by grace, God cheers each winding path he treads. A man living by grace doesn't need to work harder, accomplish more, or produce more.

It's not difficult to tell when a man is living by performance; he hides in the shadows, feeling distanced from God. I frequently encounter men who claim that they have been saved by grace, yet they have virtually no intimacy with God. When I ask them to describe their relationship with God, they describe how they feel scolded, beaten, and ashamed. They feel that they don't measure up.

Living by grace produces a different kind of man. Grace begets men who know that they measure up. Grace-oriented men sense God's love and acceptance. They feel alive, victorious, and empowered. They feel a strong attraction to God. They don't feel strong-armed into reading their Bibles or attending church. These men are drawn to the things of God.

Australia has the largest working ranches in the world. They're called cattle stations, and they dwarf our ranches in America. The largest cattle ranch in the United States, the King Ranch in Texas, has 825,000 acres. The largest cattle station in Australia, the Anna Creek Station, has 6,000,000 acres, roughly the same size as Denali National Park in Alaska.

Many of Australia's cattle stations are so large there's no way that jackaroos, Australia's ranch hands, could put up and maintain fences. Barbed wire is useless for corralling cows on a property that enormous. How do they keep their cattle from wandering off and joining other herds or disappearing forever? The jackaroos dig deep, cool artesian wells in the middle of their arid desert properties. These wells are life, and the cattle are instinctively drawn to them.

They don't need fences to keep them close. The draw to be refreshed and enlivened by the cool, clear water is enough.

People who understand grace see Jesus as a cool, clear well that provides an unending supply of life-giving refreshment. They don't need rules to keep them near God. They don't need fences. They don't need pastors, priests, or politicians to tell them to go to God. These men have tasted the water and found it to be just as refreshing as Jesus promised it would be, when He said in John 4:14: "Whoever drinks of the water that I will give him will never be thirsty again. The water that I will give him will become in him a spring of water welling up to eternal life."

FEELING GOD'S PLEASURE

Everyone benefits when men chase the right passions with unending energy. We must be spiritually healthy in order to choose the right priorities and live them well. And there's only one way for a man to be spiritually healthy: he must sense the pleasure of God, his Father. There's nothing more invigorating and energizing than when a man senses that God is delighted with him.

My son, Aidan, loves to play outside after it rains. When he hears that first drop smack the tin roof of our lean-to, there's something in his little man-spirit that revs up. His little legs begin to twitch as he stands by the window, making plans to sling mud and jump in puddles when the rain stops.

To illustrate how living by grace is more life-giving than living by performance, let's pretend that I don't want Aidan to get muddy. (This is completely hypothetical—I believe boys were designed to get muddy as often as possible.) For sake of discussion, let's say that cleanliness is a deeply held, long-standing value in the Pipher family.

Imagine me calling Aidan inside after a morning of playing outside after a rain. He walks through the back door, and he's caked in mud, head to toe. If Aidan lived in the Performance Story, the next few moments might go something like this: I yell at him and tell him how disappointed I am. "Piphers don't get muddy! What kind of a Pipher are you?" Then I discipline him, kick open the back door, and sternly say, "Get back out there and play the rest of the afternoon, but you'd better not get muddy again, or you'll really get it."

That's how it works in the Performance Story. Aidan knows that he's accepted or not based on how well he stays clean. He reaps what he sows, so when he came in muddy, he knew he'd face my wrath. He expected to see disappointment and anger in my eyes. That's what he got, because that's what he deserved.

Imagine what Aidan felt when I sent him outside again, still covered in mud. I think he'd feel all sorts of toxic motivations and feelings. He'd already feel dirty, so why avoid mud? He'd feel ashamed and embarrassed and aware that he disappoints me, so why try to do better? Any desire to do better would be driven by fear or worry that he wouldn't measure up.

That's the Performance Story. It's exhausting. This way of living certainly doesn't infuse us with a sense of freedom or energy to explore and be who we're meant to be. I can't imagine men not wanting to give it up.

Now, let's picture how that moment might look if Aidan lived in the Grace Story. Once again, he walks through the back door slathered with mud. He sees me and knows that he's failed to live up to my expectations. But rather than shoot him an expression that tells him he's a failure in my eyes, I do something shocking: I hug him. I kneel down and take him in my arms, and when I do this, all of his mud transfers onto me. When he steps back from my embrace, he's cleaner than he'd have been if he'd taken a thousand showers.

My son now stands before me spotless but still expecting discipline. He's violated my rule, and justice demands punishment. But in the Grace Story, I don't chastise him. I take the discipline that was meant for him, and I bear it myself.

Afterward, I'm facing a spotless six-year-old boy who's perfectly worthy to be my son. He doesn't need to feel guilty, ashamed, or afraid of punishment. He's clean. He's perfect. I'm pleased with him, and he sees this in my eyes.

Imagine how Aidan would feel when I sent him back outside, saying, "Aidan, you are a Pipher, and I couldn't be prouder of you. You fully measure up, and there's nothing you can do to jeopardize my love and acceptance. Go out, have fun, and stay clean. But know that when you get dirty again, *and you will get dirty again,* all you need to do is come inside and ask for forgiveness. You'll always find it. You'll always be fully loved and accepted because of what I've done for you."

That's the Grace Story. This is what God, through His son, did for us: He removed the need for us to perform well in order to earn His acceptance. We'll always have it, because Jesus earned it for us.

Which of these two stories—performance or grace—would produce the pleasure of a clean conscience? Which option would remove all of the twisted-up motivations of guilt and shame and replace them with the passion to live life to the fullest? Which would make my son feel loved and valued and, in turn, produce in him a desire to be with me?

Living by grace is the extreme, most life-giving pursuit, because it sends men out filled with energy, zeal, and the desire to race into new adventures with healthy motivations.

GRACE VERSUS PERFORMANCE IN *CHARIOTS OF FIRE*

Chariots of Fire is my favorite movie largely because of how well it contrasts a man living by grace with a man living by performance.

This movie tells the story of two men, Eric Liddell and Harold Abrahams, who run for Great Britain in the 1924 Olympic Games in Paris. Liddell is a Christian, who understands that his identity isn't dependent on how well he performs. God fully accepts him, and he accepts himself, because of Jesus's life and death. Abrahams, on the other hand, fights the world for respect. He believes that his value is entirely dependent on his performance on the track.

Throughout the movie, Eric Liddell's inner peace is juxtaposed with Harold Abrahams's inner turmoil. You can see the condition of their hearts in their running style. Liddell runs with a smile on his face, his arms bouncing and spinning as he glides across the track in a relaxed stride. His eyes are fixed in a distant stare, giving a sense that he's thinking of deeper, more wonderful things than simply winning the race. Watching Liddell's character run in *Chariots of Fire* gives me a sense that the grace of God pats him on the back and nudges him forward with ease.

Watching Abrahams run gives me a sense that the gnarly fists of performance keep slapping him in the face, slamming him in the stomach, and pounding his thighs. His face is scrunched up in anxiety and stress. Abrahams is not staring off into something deeper; he's looking to his side with panic in his eyes. Instead of being carried forward by the grace of God, Abrahams is pushing against his own critical expectations and standards. He believes he's battling the world and its prejudice, but he has no greater enemy than his desire to feel that he measures up based on how well he performs.

Even when Abrahams wins, he has no joy. The most depressing scene in the movie takes place after Abrahams claims an unexpected victory in the hundred-meter dash at the Olympics. He goes to a bar with his trainer, Sam Mussabini, gets drunk, and then sinks into a deep, sulking depression. Abrahams's victory was empty, because a win on the track did not justify his existence as he had hoped it would.

Liddell also wins his event, the 400-meter dash. However, unlike Abrahams, Liddell runs the race with a sense of the pleasure of God. He's in a different dimension. It doesn't matter if he wins or loses, or how anyone else does, or who's watching; Liddell is catapulted forward, one lighthearted step after another, by the sense that his Father loves and accepts him. He wins. He does perform well. But he runs hard and wins as a result of knowing that he pleases God, not as a means of trying to earn God's acceptance.

To live by grace is to move back into the picture of perfect significance and satisfaction in Genesis chapter 2. Because of an infinitely perfect person who lived and died on our behalf, we measure up. This reality cannot be touched. Other people might attack us. The world might call us fools. Our enemies might throw sticks and stones and call us names that wound. But they cannot touch our self-worth and significance. If God is pleased with us, we have nothing to fear. The Apostle Paul writes in Romans 8:31, "If God is for us, who can be against us?"

Jesus said, "I came that they may have life and have it abundantly" (John 10:10). Those weren't empty words. Jesus was inviting people into something bigger, something more significant than the Performance Story. He was giving an invitation to an indescribable life with those words.

All we have to do is reach out and accept it.

As a gift.

**Be more concerned with your character than
your reputation, because your character is
what you really are, while your reputation is
merely what others think you are.**

—JOHN WOODEN

6

AN INTERNAL COMPASS

When I was in ninth grade, I qualified to be on the varsity swim team. I was one of three gangly junior-high kids who carpooled from the tiny confines of Irving Middle School to the vast, mature campus of Southeast High School. I didn't look cool, but I sure felt it.

This honor was not without a cost. To join the team, I had to swim the infamous "Gauntlet." On the first day of practice, I stepped out of the locker room to see all of the varsity swimmers in the pool, holding kickboards, giving me stares of death. Good feelings gone, I wanted to take my towel, swim cap, and goggles and hide underneath the bleachers.

There was no escape. This was a rite of passage that every varsity swimmer had gone through for at least ten years, and they weren't about to let me opt out. Two seniors got out of the pool, circled behind me, and escorted me to the pool. I took a deep breath, dove in, and swam fifty yards through two lines of bloodthirsty upperclassmen using kickboards to create massive waves of water. It took me about sixty seconds to swim the

Gauntlet, a solid minute of being force-fed chlorinated water. The Gauntlet broke my goggles, sent my suit to my knees, and made me throw up in the gutter.

WAVES WITHOUT AND WITHIN

Most men navigate a gauntlet every day. From the moment they sit up in bed and put their feet on the floor until the time they plug in their cell phones at the end of the night, they're hit from all sides with opportunities and demands. Men face hundreds of decisions a day. Decisions about where to spend their time, energy, and resources. Decisions that challenge their values. Decisions that test and prove their character. The waves hit us from all directions.

My work as a pastor can be dangerously consuming. Ministry never ends. There's no set start or finish time to a day. Pastoral work is never done, because people never stop needing to be nurtured or experiencing medical, spiritual, and relational emergencies. Ministry takes as much from me as I'm willing to give. Many men feel this about their careers. Work feels perpetually unfinished.

So does home. Last I checked, my house wasn't equipped with a time clock and punch cards. (Note to self.) There's no stopping point to the daily work of being a husband and father. There's always one more book to read to the kids, one more repair to make, and one more important issue to talk through. Like work, home gladly receives whatever time and energy men will give it.

There's a lot of pressure on men today to adopt smallish, empty ideas of what manhood looks like. If a man has a hundred family members, friends, and coworkers, he has a hundred opinions to sift through. This means that men continually wrestle with the questions *What does it look like to be the best possible version of me? Am I going to be true to myself, or am I going to settle for someone else's expectations for my life?*

Sometimes our peer groups, even our friends, encourage us to be something less than we should be. I recently counseled a farmer from our community, Stuart, after he found out his wife had kissed another man at her workplace. Stuart's friends were coaching him in one direction, but his conscience didn't agree. During the first session, Stuart asked me, "What should I do? My friends keep telling me to dump her, but I don't think I could do that."

"Dump" a wife after fifteen years of marriage? What a horrible idea. If Stuart had followed his friends' advice, he would surely have experienced even deeper degrees of pain. Instead, Stuart chose to stay in the marriage. He asked his wife to go to counseling with him, and they've been moving forward in a positive direction these past six months.

One of the persistent voices that encourage men to chase tiny, disastrous dreams comes from the marketing industry. Billboards, advertisements, and commercials constantly slam men with messages that are truly counter to their deepest priorities. The message marketed by most companies is that men will feel significant only if they purchase their products.

For example, Dodge ran an advertisement during the 2010 Super Bowl that tried to convince men that because they pander to everyone in all areas of their lives, they deserve to drive the car they want. The first part of the commercial pictured men with expressionless, compliant faces, while a man's voice ticked through a list of all the things men do to make other people happy: waking up at 6:30 to walk the dog, being civil to their mothers-in-law, and putting the seat down after they pee. Men are portrayed as little more than emasculated lap dogs for the first fifty seconds of this commercial.

Then, in the last ten seconds, a car engine roars like a jet engine, and the man's voice (finally) fills with vigor and conviction as he declares, "And because I do this . . . I will drive the car I want to drive."

That's a telling commercial on several levels. First of all, if Dodge is on target, then a common trend among men is the feeling that life consists primarily of doing meaningless, menial tasks in order to please other people. A man doing only as he's told is a pretty empty picture of manhood. In one of his essays, Wendell Berry describes how people tend to admire tough, independent, free-thinking men. However, Berry explains, there aren't many exemplars to choose from; many men have traded the life of rugged individuality for the life of saying yes in order to make a paycheck.

Berry writes: "But despite their he-man pretensions and their captivation by masculine heroes of sports, war, and the Old West, most men are now entirely accustomed to obeying and currying the favor of their bosses. Because of this, of course, they hate their jobs—they mutter, 'Thank God it's Friday' and 'Pretty good for Monday'—but they do as they are told."[1]

If Dodge's research team has drawn the right conclusions, we've got a lot of do-as-they-are-told men in America these days.

This commercial is also an example of a small, empty idea in a sea of thousands of such ideas that continually challenge men's values and priorities. The message went something like this: "Guys, because you cater to other people all day long, pleasing everyone but yourselves, you deserve to spend an outrageous amount of money on a car that will finally give you a sense of significance. So take out a loan, buy a Charger, and hold fast to that last, tiny, frayed-out strand of your manhood."

Perhaps I'm off base here, but I'm guessing that most men would need to take out a loan in order to purchase a new Charger. This would plunge them deeper into debt, chaining them even more tightly to the pander-to-others-to-make-a-buck hamster wheel. The end result: these men would need to work more hours, spend less time with their family and friends, and say more often, "Yes, sir. I'll do that for you." All to pay off the loan for the shiny red Charger sitting long hours in a work parking lot.

Is that the "Ram Toughness" we want for our men? Is that the picture of significance and manhood we want to adopt?

I'm unfairly picking on Dodge here; they are just one of hundreds of companies that drop millions of dollars a year miseducating men. I should give these companies a bit of credit. Their commercials *do* work. They're enticing. What man wouldn't like to rip off his tie at the end of a mundane day, throw on some shorts and sunglasses, and then hit the open road in a jerk-your-head-back-fast sports car?

These sophisticated appeals to our deepest desires confuse men as they try to make good decisions throughout their days. I often finish my days wiped out. By the time I hit the pillow, the only thing more exhausted than my body is my mind. On any given day, I feel tested, tried, pushed, pulled, and run over by the opportunities and demands I've fielded. Decisions come at a cost. Even when we make healthy choices, such as not divorcing a wife of fifteen years, or not staking our sense of manhood on a Dodge Charger, they still take their toll. Some mornings, when I wake up and survey the landscape of my upcoming day, I just want to take my cap and goggles and go hide under the bleachers.

THE COMPASS OF CHARACTER

But curling up in the fetal position under the bleachers isn't an option. Men must get out of bed, get dressed, and navigate the plethora of choices each day presents. As hard as decision making can be, though, there is help. There is something that helps clarify the best options from the lesser ones. It's called character.

Dallas Willard provides a helpful definition of character in his book *Renovation of the Heart.* Willard defines character as the "internal, overall structure of the self that is revealed by our long-run patterns of behavior and from which our actions more or less automatically arise."[2]

According to Willard's definition, character can be good or bad, moral or immoral, consistent or inconsistent. Each man has some form of character, some type of internal organization of the soul that determines how he'll act most of the time.

We can observe character in others. This is precisely what we're doing when we evaluate credit reports, résumés, letters of reference, and reputations; we are trying to determine "what kind of thoughts, feelings, and tendencies of will that person habitually acts from, and therefore how he or she will act in the future."[3]

Few things inspire me more than a display of consistent, God-centered character. Another reason that *Chariots of Fire* is my favorite movie is that it paints a clear picture of Eric Liddell's strength of character. Character is often tested in the crucible of high-pressure situations, moments like the one Liddell encountered shortly after withdrawing from the 100-meter dash. Liddell's participation in the 100-meter was Britain's greatest chance at gold, but the opening heats were scheduled for a Sunday. Liddell's conviction was that Sunday was the Lord's day and not a day to play sports. He was placed in a seemingly impossible predicament. Earlier in the movie, he'd shared that conviction with a young boy who was playing soccer on the Sabbath. Now it was his turn to decide whether he would remain true to what he believed or cave in to the pressure to please Great Britain.

The British Olympic committee, including the Prince of Wales and the Duke of Sutherland, invited Liddell to meet with them. Behind closed doors, Britain's top officials tried numerous tactics to persuade him to run. He was visibly uncomfortable and agitated.

He was also immovable. Liddell was able to discern the right choice, the option that would not violate his conscience, and then exert the will to carry it out. His difficult decision was made simple by his internal compass. When faced with multiple options, all he needed to do was look inside, into his convictions and values, and make the best choice.

I recently read about another man who followed his convictions and made a difficult, countercultural decision. Francis Chan, the pastor of Cornerstone Community Church in Simi Valley, California, decided that the people around him were too focused on him and not enough on Jesus. "Even in my own church I heard the words 'Francis Chan' more than I heard the words 'Holy Spirit,'" Chan said.[4]

Chan was a bestselling author. His church had four thousand members. He was a popular event speaker. Many men would look at this leader and say, "He's arrived." However, these things didn't feed Chan's ego; they deeply concerned him. When he sensed that his ministry had become too much about Francis Chan, he decided it was time to disappear. As Eric Marrapodi wrote on CNN's Belief Blog, "there apparently is no hidden scandal, no money trail, and no 'other' woman." Chan's internal compass signaled to him that it was time for a break.

THE DRIVING QUESTION OF CHARACTER

The remainder of this book will examine some of the key relationships and priorities that ambitious, pursuit-driven men must honor if they hope to live well. The upcoming chapters will explore marriage, parenting, friendships, and pursuing other dreams. There are hundreds of opinions and perspectives on these subjects. Friends have opinions. Hollywood presents numerous perspectives. Our churches, families, and coworkers consistently voice their ideas about how we should live. Men often feel pressure to run in various directions.

For a man to have a strong, consistent character, he must resolve the question *Who do I most want to please with my life?* A machismo man might object, stating, "I don't live to please anyone! I'm my own man." That answer reveals that man is living to please himself, but it still proves the point that all men live to please someone. The key to strong character is figuring out *who* that person should be.

The Apostle Paul resolved this question for himself, and it steeled his character. In 1 Corinthians, Paul addressed the expectations that the church in Corinth had for him. Paul was swimming his own gauntlet through that community, receiving wave after wave of criticism and pressure to conform. The issue was rhetoric, or speaking ability. Rhetoric was extremely important in that first-century culture. Much the way Nebraska fans cheer and criticize the Cornhuskers football team, Corinth held high hopes and strong expectations for its best orators.

Paul didn't want to base his actions and message on pleasing others. That didn't prevent his followers from placing expectations on him. All men feel the pressure to conform and perform, and Paul was no exception. What was exceptional was Paul's inner compass. He had resolved to live for God's approval *alone,* and this resolution gave him clarity when he felt pressure from others.

Paul writes, "But with me it is a very small thing that I should be judged by you or by any human court. In fact, I do not even judge myself. For I am not aware of anything against myself, but I am not thereby acquitted. It is the Lord who judges me" (1 Corinthians 4:3–4).

Paul's own opinion of himself wasn't his priority. The Corinthians' opinions weren't what mattered most. Paul lived to be faithful to God alone. This clarity, this resolution, enabled Paul to face the most intense pressure with direction, with conviction. It wasn't easy for Paul to experience the pressure, but he had a clear and accessible paradigm for making the right choice.

What an inspiring, challenging picture of integrity for us in a day when men take out car loans to try to enhance their image and sense of self-worth. Paul stands as a man among men because he would not cave. He was determined to honor Jesus Christ, even if nobody else approved.

Every man can have this compass for his life. The resolve to be faithful to God above all others simplifies and clarifies the most intense, high-pressured decisions he will face. By saying "simplify" and "clarify," I'm not implying that men's decisions will be easy or that life will be free of stress. The most internally organized man will still experience a battle inside to make the best choices. Strong character doesn't make difficult decisions easy. Strong character gives men a quickly accessible paradigm for making the best choice.

Here is how resolving to be faithful to God makes decisions simpler and clearer: Whether a man faces a smaller decision of his day or a larger, life-defining one, he only needs to find the best answer to one question: *What does God want from me?*

The answer to that question does not always come quickly. It's not always clear. It will often require searching convictions, the Scriptures, and the counsel of trusted friends and family. What makes this question simpler and easier *isn't* that the answer is easy to find but rather that we're only trying to find one answer, one person's opinion.

Consider the man who hasn't made a commitment to honor God above all others. This man will tend to struggle with decision making. His process becomes more complicated, fractured. Before making a decision, this man will first need to choose whom he most hopes to please. Sometimes he'll choose to do his boss's bidding. Quite often, his wife's expectations will sit in the driver's seat. At other times, his friends will determine his course.

In all decisions, the man who hasn't determined to honor the Lord with each decision will resort to making decisions based largely on feelings. *What do I feel like doing?* becomes the fallback question for making choices.

What do I feel like doing? is a dangerous question when it comes to decision making. It's dangerous because men will often choose the option that is the most *fun*. After a hard day at work, watching television is more fun than helping a child with homework. On a Saturday afternoon, rock climbing is more fun than paying bills or mowing the lawn. It's more fun to play cards with friends than it is to help decorate the Christmas tree with the family.

With each decision, there is usually a *fun option*, and as men, we are masterfully good at recognizing it. However, what is most fun is often not what is most important. The fun option is not necessarily the regret-free option. I was reminded of this a couple of nights ago. It was the Saturday after Thanksgiving, and the day we planned to put up our Christmas tree.

Oh, but I wanted to duck hunt. While Jamie and the kids carried boxes of ornaments and lights up from the basement, I checked the wind direction and made plans for how to set up the decoys. About two o'clock in the afternoon, my children noticed that I was gathering my hunting clothing. My son blurted out, "Dad, what are you doing? Aren't you going to help us decorate the tree?"

I presented several well-reasoned arguments for why they didn't need me to help decorate. I reminded them that, technically, I've never really helped decorate our Christmas trees. Sure, I cut the bottom of the trunk off, carry the tree into the house, and set it up in the base. But from that point on, I reminded them, they've always decorated the tree with their mom. Most years, I sit by the fire, drink hot chocolate, and cheer them on as they climb the little footstool and hang the ornaments.

I walked them through this airtight argument for why they

should let me have fun and duck hunt and then made the statement, "So, you see, you won't even know I'm gone."

My older daughter sighed and said, "OK, Dad. You should go hunting." The other two agreed, and they all went back to decorating.

When they turned their backs to me to hang the next ornament, a feeling of sadness settled into my chest. I had won, but it felt as if I'd lost. Did I really want my family to give up on my presence? Would small concessions in moments like this lead to a larger giving up on me down the road? I've known men whose families had given up on them—was this how it happens?

The questions haunted me for a few moments.

I've made the wrong decision many times but not that afternoon. A few moments after my children reluctantly "set me free" to have fun, I realized that this was not the kind of dad I wanted to be. More important than that, this was not the kind of dad that God wanted me to be. I stayed home, made a fire in the fireplace, and cheered my family on as they transformed that eight-foot tree into a gigantic, brilliant fire hazard.

Men who live to please others or their own feelings are fragmented inside, unsure of themselves. Their multiple desires and lack of focus will make them miserable. I certainly know this experience firsthand. Before I turned my life over to Jesus during my sophomore year in college, the worst part of every decision was trying to determine whom I most wanted to please or appease. A simple decision such as how to spend an evening could become exhausting. *Do I study for my test so that I can try to impress my teacher? Do I hang out with my friends in my dorm so that they like me and I feel included in their lives? Do I give in and go for a jog with my roommate who's been asking me for weeks to tag along? Do I hang out with my girlfriend who has been asking for more of my time lately?* All of these options appealed, because all of these options would please other people. Yet all of these options posed the risk of letting other people down.

Eventually, I'd go with my gut and make my best choice. Then, quite often, I'd second-guess myself the entire evening, thinking about the other people I could have pleased had I made a different choice. I lived the misery of a fragmented life.

No more.

This morning, a man came into church and wanted to talk about the sermon I had preached on Sunday. I poured Jim a mug of coffee as he told me that my preaching wasn't his cup of tea. Jim had grown up in a different denomination and had hoped that my style of preaching would have been more like the style of his former pastor. Jim is just one of many people I've talked with recently about my preaching. One man asked me to speak about global warming and our role as a church in the environmental movement. Another couple told me that they would like to hear me be more charismatic—animated—when I speak. Another man, with tears in his eyes, told me that my sermons presented the grace of God in a way that he'd never heard before. He gave me a hug and said, "Keep doing what you're doing, Pastor."

How should I preach? What should I emphasize? What style should I take in the pulpit? If I tried to answer these questions based on what would please other people, I'd be the most sensitive, thin-skinned, flaky pastor in America this coming Sunday morning. The response of people would matter too much. My focus would shift entirely onto my performance as judged by my parishioners. I'd be an insecure mess.

However, if I search my conscience, study the Scriptures,

and walk to the podium with a desire simply to please God, I experience an inner strength and sense of direction that nobody can threaten.

All men can have this simple and clear decision-making paradigm. All it takes is a desire to be faithful to God above all the other voices and opinions. All it takes is keeping our eyes fixed on Jesus Christ and His purposes and plans for us.

THE PAINTED BLACK LINE

On that first day of swim practice, as I tried to navigate through the hostile waves of the Gauntlet, the hardest part was moving forward and finishing. When two rows of varsity swimmers use kickboards to create typhoon-size swells, it's easy to lose your bearings. As a scrawny, 120-pound kid, I got tossed to the side, spun around, and pushed under for several moments at a time.

What kept me moving forward and eventually enabled me to finish was the black line at the bottom of the pool. I could be flipped and flopped in a number of directions, but if I could re-acquire that stripe in my sights, I could get back on course.

Over my next four years, I got to know that black line intimately. I logged somewhere between 100,000 and 150,000 yards a season, swimming up and down that pool, staring at that painted black line. I focused on that line every time the starter yelled, "Swimmers, take your mark!" I used that line to reposition myself every time I did a flip turn. The line told me how close I was to the wall, the finish line. That line kept me moving forward for four years. The image of that line is still burned in my brain today.

To live truly well, as men of strong character and purpose,

we must keep our eyes fixed on Jesus Christ. Pleasing Him must be our resolve. When we consider our marriages, our parenting, our friendships, and our other priorities and pursuits, we should have no higher goal than faithfulness to Jesus. Honoring God is the black line. A man who burns the question *What does God want from me?* into his mind, so that it becomes his mode of operation, is a man prepared to live and finish well in these key relationships and priorities we're about to examine.

He who loves his wife loves himself.

—PAUL THE APOSTLE

7

THE FAMILIAR TOUCH OF
THE LONG-MARRIED

For years, I'd tell my wife that she was more important
than my hobbies and pursuits.

For years, she had her doubts.

Jamie and I have had dozens of arguments about what held
the largest part of my heart, her or my pursuits. These "discussions" weren't fun for either of us. I'd reassure her over and
over that she was my highest priority, and then I couldn't understand why she doubted me. She'd try to articulate her skep-
ticism but couldn't quite put it into words. This cycle repeated
itself every hunting, fishing, and golfing season for the first few
years of our marriage.

A couple of years ago, like participants in a three-legged
race, we stumbled across the answer. I was moments away from
leaving home to drive to Missouri to deer hunt for three days. I
had my packing list in hand, directions printed out, and all of
my gear meticulously packed in the truck. I'd stayed up until
two o'clock the night before making sure that every aspect of

my hunt was planned well. Before pulling out of the drive-way, I'd hopped out of the cab and run inside for one more kiss good-bye.

I leaned in and puckered up. Jamie pulled back a bit and asked, "Did you line up a babysitter for our date on Saturday?"

A lump formed in the back of my throat. "Um . . . no, I didn't. Could you get one for us?" I said sheepishly.

Noticeably irritated, she asked, "What *do* you have planned for our date, anyway? You promised that we'd do something special."

Even I am amazed at the stupidity of what I said next. "To be honest, I haven't given it much thought."

The nine-year fog of not quite understanding each other evaporated in the moments that followed. Jamie suddenly found the perfect words to communicate her feelings.

"That's it! That's exactly why I feel like you value hunting more than me! You've spent a month planning every detail of this archery hunt but didn't spend five minutes on our date Saturday night. Tell me . . . why shouldn't I feel like hunting is more important to you?"

When I was fifteen, someone dared me to wrestle an eigh-teen-year-old state champion wrestler after school. The entire ordeal was over in about three seconds. That Herculean upper-classman had nothing on my wife; her question pinned me in a third of that time. I'm a word person. My degree is in com-munication. I spend most of my hours each week drafting and combining words for effective writing, preaching, and counsel-ing. I'm rarely stuck without something to say. Yet Jamie's ques-tion left me speechless.

We stared at each other for a long moment. Then I swallowed hard, crossed the kitchen floor, and hugged her. I told her I was sorry and that I understood how she felt. She believed me and hugged me back.

Why it took nine years to understand my wife's feelings, I have no idea. But for some reason, in that moment, I finally realized that my words counted for very little when my actions didn't back them up.

A FAIR QUESTION

Wives study their husbands. They watch how their husbands interact with their interests and pursuits. They pay attention to the amount of time men spend reading *Runner's World* or fiddling with recreational equipment or sitting in boats or tree stands. They notice the excitement in their husbands' voices when they talk about the trips they have planned. They see the dollars that their husbands are happy to drop on a new set of golf clubs or the latest cell phone. Wives watch closely. They're trying to discern what their husbands love and how much. What a wife is really trying to figure out is *When it comes to my husband's heart, how do I measure up compared with everything else?*

It's a fair question. A bit painful, perhaps. But fair. What makes it a legitimate question is that when a man gives himself to his wife in marriage, in a very real sense, he becomes her possession. That probably sounds like an odd way to state it, but this is what a man is saying when he makes the vow "to have and to hold from this day forward."

The Bible talks about this shared ownership in passages

such as 1 Corinthians 7:4: "For the wife does not have authority over her own body, but the husband does. Likewise the husband does not have authority over his own body, but the wife does." Men share possession of their wives, and wives share possession of their husbands. This is marital intimacy, and it's the commitment implied with the simple, two-word phrase "I do."

Mike Mason celebrates the idea that a husband and wife share ownership of each other in his book *The Mystery of Marriage*. He writes: "The very heart of intimacy is reached when two people are neither afraid nor ashamed of being possessed by love, when in fact they give themselves freely to the pure joy and liberty of owning and being owned." He adds, "For our identity is hidden in love, a love that cannot exist at all until it gives itself away. A robust spirit of abandonment, but equally of possessiveness, is one more of the ways in which a marriage may reflect the very attributes of God."[1]

When a husband puts a ring on his wife's finger, his wife rightfully expects that she will remain the deepest affection in his heart. She plans on being more important than a trip to the Bahamas to fish or scuba dive, more important than a membership to the gym or the country club, and more important than time spent fixing up that old car or building a career. She's been promised the top spot in her husband's affections, which means that when she suspects that someone else, or something else, has outcompeted her, it feels grossly wrong. She *rightly* feels jealous.

Wives will often use strong language to describe these feelings. I've heard dozens of wives state that a husband's top passion feels like a "mistress." One articulate wife told me in the foyer of our church, in front of her husband, "Tom may have put a ring on my finger, but he's married to his bass boat."

I didn't quite know how to reply to that one. Neither did Tom, who stood there looking down at the tile floor with a sick look on his face.

GOOD BUT DANGEROUS

Passionate men can be a gift to their families. They often take mundane moments and infuse them with laughter, enthusiasm, and a sense of adventure. Life is colorful and exciting when men are fired up inside. Many women marry men precisely because of this quality. Jamie has told me several times, "I knew life with you would never be boring, Zeke. That's one of the reasons I married you."

Women are drawn to interesting, enthusiastic, passionate men. Yet these very qualities can undermine a relationship if a man redirects his attention away from his wife toward a career or a hobby. I witnessed a tragic example of this truth last summer while I was mowing my lawn. As I cruised up and down my lawn on a riding mower, a man from our church, Drew, pulled up onto my curb, leaped from his pickup, and threw himself onto the grass in front of me. This strong, hard-working rancher wept so loudly that my neighbors stepped outside to investigate.

I killed the engine, knelt down beside him, and asked why he was in such pain. Tears streamed down his cheeks and off his beard as he explained that his wife had been having an affair. As cliché as it sounds, Drew had returned home that afternoon from working cattle to an empty house and a note on the kitchen table that said, "I moved out. This marriage was over a long time ago."

"I just want to die, I hurt so bad," Drew moaned.

I met with Drew several times over the weeks that followed. His wife, Sandy, even agreed to come in for one of those meetings. When I asked her what had caused her to leave, she said, "All he ever wanted to do was work. He's gone before the sun rises to fix a fence or work on a tractor and then comes home and works in the garage until midnight. Obviously, I never mattered to him."

Drew's work ethic and desire to provide were among the things that Sandy first noticed about him twenty years earlier. She watched Drew build the farm from scratch. Her father had been a hard worker, and she was attracted to the same quality in Drew. In the beginning of their marriage, Drew kept work in perspective. They had coffee and breakfast together every morning at the metal table in their kitchen. Drew would even ask her to join him on a horse some afternoons as he checked the herd. Early on, Sandy felt she was more important than his work.

However, somewhere along the way, the order changed, and as hard as she tried, Sandy couldn't reposition herself back at the top.

Drew promised several times during that counseling session and over the weeks that followed that he would work fewer hours and spend more time with Sandy. But it was too late.

I'm a pastor, so people include me in intimate struggles or joys. This is not only an honor; it can be deeply enjoyable. I greatly enjoy helping with baby dedications, weddings, and baptisms. Yet there are moments so painful, so tragic, that watching others go through them wipes *me* out. At the top of this list, sharing the spot with untimely deaths and church splits, are broken marriages. Drew and Sandy's divorce depressed me for weeks.

THE CHALLENGE

As this world spins like a merry-go-round at more than a thousand miles per hour, marriages get flung off at an alarming rate. It always surprises us when this happens. A man who slips a band onto a woman's finger never expects to get that ring back someday. Nobody enters into marriage planning to separate. Each time I do premarital counseling with an eager, optimistic couple, I ask them, "Do you think there's any chance that divorce is an option down the road?"

Every time, without fail, the couple retorts, "Absolutely not! That will *never* happen to us."

Yet, sadly, it often does. Approximately 33 percent of the time.[2]

Marriage is difficult. Yank your teeth out without Novocain difficult. The best marriages face conflict, stress, and pressure. However, marriages that involve a pursuit-driven man face a unique challenge: passionate men are easily pulled away from higher priorities by lesser ones. When this happens, they tend to orient their other relationships and priorities *behind* these pursuits.

When I ask men if they've put a pursuit ahead of their wives, the answer is usually "No, I love my wife and tell her that all the time." However, priorities that are stated but not

lived out are not priorities. When men demonstrate more enthusiasm toward their hobbies than they do toward their marriages, trite statements of affection stop meaning much.

Wives who sense that they've been prioritized below a pursuit or career are often overly sensitive about their husbands'
pursuits. I heard many men complain about their wives' critical attitudes toward their hobbies. What men need to realize is
that the critical attitude is not entirely the wives' fault. Men who
promise to cherish their wives above all things but then go out
and put hobbies and interests above their spouses are inviting
conflict.

THE GENEROUS, CHERISHED WIFE

While a *devalued* wife tends to feel extra-sensitive, a *cherished*
wife tends to be extra-secure. A secure, deeply loved wife will
tend to be a generous, other-centered wife. There's a fascinating
statement in the book of Ephesians that provides helpful direction to husbands. The Apostle Paul writes: "He who loves his
wife loves himself" (Ephesians 5:28b).

I'd read that statement dozens of times before Jamie finally
helped me understand it. After the epiphany moment before
my hunting trip to Missouri, Jamie said something to me that
I'll never forget. She said, "Zeke, I think I can be a great wife
for you. I have no desire to stand in the way of your pursuits.
I'm simple, in this sense: as long as I know that you cherish me
more than your work and hobbies, I'll be very accommodating.
Supportive."

Jamie was echoing the truth that Paul had written about
two thousand years earlier. She was telling me that if I loved

her well, the way a husband ought to cherish his wife, things would go very well for me. If she felt secure, happy, and deeply loved, I would also experience satisfaction and pleasure in my marriage.

One of the greatest lies that the Devil ever told was that people give up pleasure when they choose to honor God. Adam and Eve ate the fruit from the tree of the knowledge of good and evil because they believed that if they didn't, they'd be missing out on something *better*. Are people that different today? It seems that we believe that same lie today, when we assume that unless we put ourselves ahead of others, we won't find happiness. This just isn't the case. In fact, it couldn't be further from the truth. Passionate men who cherish and adore their wives are the happiest of men. What's more, it's often their wives who make sure of their happiness.

I believe this idea so strongly that the first thing I tell a young man who is heading toward marriage is that he's got an opportunity to treat *himself* really, really well. All he needs to do is make sure to keep his wife at the top of his priority list, showing her that she's more important than any job, hobby, sport, or other relationship. I tell the young man with love in his eyes that if he'll do that, his wife will likely be the most generous, gracious person in his life. Who doesn't want to spend forty, perhaps sixty years with a generous, gracious person sleeping, eating, and walking by his side?

TWO IMAGES, TWO CHOICES

I carry two images in my mind when I think about marriage and finishing life well. These pictures come from the world of outdoor writing. I consider these images as the two potential paths I can choose to walk down.

The first is an outdoor writer who's had more success in the field than 95 percent of all sportsmen. I will never need a trophy room as large as this man already requires, and he's not done hunting yet. He's had unparalleled success in the forests and fields of a dozen countries. His articles are published regularly in every major outdoor journal. He pays for nothing; outdoor-gear companies and outfitters call him and beg him to use their products. To many young, aspiring hunters and outdoor writers, this man appears to be living the dream.

Yet he's burned through two marriages and is finishing life alone in a palace of exotic trophies. When he slips into bed, there's not another set of toes waiting to warm his up. When he makes a pot of coffee in the morning, only one mug comes down off the shelf. He buys one ticket at the movie theater. This man is lonely and plagued by feelings of regret. I know this man, and his life cautions me.

His life also makes the second picture more attractive. My friend Charlie is a sportsman and outdoor writer in his early sixties. In my opinion, he's a success in every sense of the word. He's been married to the same woman for forty years. Together, they live in upstate New York, enjoy a close relationship with their son, and share a life brimming with pleasant memories. On his worst day afield, when sixty-mile-an-hour Canadian winds strike from the north, piercing his jacket and chilling his bones, Charlie still finishes every photo shoot and bow-hunt happy. His frozen face smiles the entire way back to the truck, because he knows he's returning to soup waiting on the stove, a fire in the fireplace, and a wife who adores him and can't wait to hear about his day.

Charlie's living the dream. The *real* dream. Mark Twain writes, "Love seems the swiftest, but it is the slowest of all growths. No man or woman really knows what perfect love is until they have been married a quarter of a century." Charlie and his wife, Carla, surpass Twain's benchmark by fifteen years.

Jamie makes our home warm, even when the unimpeded Nebraska winds howl across the prairie and rattle the lead-paned windows of our one-hundred-year-old home. On frigid, blustery nights, it sounds as if a dozen people are whistling from underneath the floorboards of our house. Yet Jamie's laugh, her love for the kids, and her enjoyment of books, friends, and good food keep our life toasty.

Jamie and I like a poem, "After Making Love We Hear Footsteps," by Galway Kinnell. Jamie found this poem several years ago and gave it to me in an anniversary card. Both of us pull it out periodically and read it to each other. We tell each other that this poem paints a picture of the life we have and want to have.

There's one phrase in Kinnell's poem that we've particularly latched on to: the "familiar touch of the long-married." After thirteen years of marriage, Jamie and I have lived in four cities, we've given life to three children, and I've graduated from two seminaries. We've traveled together to Ireland, England, Scotland, Israel, Kazakhstan, and China. In each other's presence, we've snored, wept, aged, and learned to be parents, lovers, and friends. Each of us could list with frightening accuracy the other person's flaws (for the record, Jamie would need more ink in her pen), while affirming our complete devotion to each other. After thirteen years of marriage, we've only begun to glimpse the pleasures of the long-married that Charlie and Carla enjoy.

But I want more. A lot more. I want to know what it feels like to be married to Jamie for a quarter of a century and then beyond. I want to be a part of that fraternity of contented, warmhearted men who hit long-married status. But I'm aware that to reach long-married status, I've got my work cut out for me.

A GOOD THING

If a man desires to have a strong, healthy, enjoyable marriage, he must work at it. Long-married status will not happen accidentally. It's earned. It's attained. It's fought for. A man must pursue the long-married vision with more fervor and zeal than he puts toward every other pursuit, hobby, or career in his life. Achieving a good marriage is like ice-picking your way up a frozen mountain; it's difficult, sometimes painful work that requires constant movement. The moment you stop climbing, quit trying, and take a break, things get cold. Cold is deadly.

However, if you keep moving forward, keep growing and changing and learning to put your wife first, the heat stays. Heat is life-giving. One of my favorite singer-songwriters, Andrew Peterson, describes marriage perfectly. In his song "Love Is a Good Thing," Peterson celebrates the irony of how a great, loving marriage will summon from you everything you have to give, but it's worth it. He sings, "It knocked me down, it dragged me out, it left me there for dead. It took all the freedom I wanted and gave me something else instead. It blew my mind, it bled me dry, it hit me like a long good-bye, and nobody here knows better than I that it's a good thing. Love is a good thing."

Having a set of toes waiting to tickle yours at night is a good thing. Filling up two coffee mugs in the morning is a good thing. Finishing life with a companion of forty or perhaps sixty years is a good, good thing. So good that it's worth every effort and sacrifice we can give to make it happen.

When my kids become wild and unruly, I use a nice, safe playpen. When they're finished, I climb out.

—ERMA BOMBECK

8

MONKEYS AT THE ZOO

Most days, when I come home from work, there's at least one smell I can't identify.

Sometimes it's a sippy cup with mysterious green fluid lurking under the couch. Other times it's the dank smell of sweaty clothing that's been balled up and stuffed back into a drawer. Occasionally, it's the stench from a pet "deposit" in our yard that the kids have tracked into the house. Our home is never without smells.

Sometimes the smells are the best parts of home. One scent I enjoy even more than vanilla or baked bread is spring's fresh air when it's settled into my children's hair after hours of playing outside. When I catch that scent, I'll often grab their heads for long moments, hold them under my nose, and state over and over, "No, you can't leave yet. I'm not done sniffing your noggin."

Smells come with the territory. So do noises.

A herd of elk crashing through the timber can't compare to the ruckus my children can make. This morning, it was Aidan building towers out of tin cans in order to create new methods of demolishing them. It was the clamor of Claire running up and down the rickety pine floors of the attic, trying on one dress after another and then yelling at the top of her lungs, "*Now* do I look like a princess?" It was also Kate, our eldest, laughing out loud as she read a book by the fireplace. These were some of the noises of this morning, but each day brings new chaos of its own.

However, I'll have to admit that the sights, smells, and noises of home contribute to my love of the outdoors. I'm often drawn to the water at sundown to escape the chaos, if even for an hour. When I'm standing on the deck of a bass boat in the middle of a lake, the only smells that pass through my nostrils are fresh air and lake water. The only noises I hear are the zinging of my line unspooling and the slap of the popper hitting the surface. Occasionally, the welcome commotion of a bass slamming my top-water lure and zipping out my line fills my ears with pleasure.

The lakes and forests of Nebraska are often the only arenas where I find the peace and quiet I knew nine years ago, during the pre-kids stage of our marriage. Home is now a monkey cage. My kids have *zooified* that domain. I'm thirty-nine and in the throes of fatherhood—the fast-paced, most difficult, yet most rewarding stage of a man's life.

Not that fathers ever stop parenting, but the years when our sons and daughters are under our roofs disappear from sight faster than a flock of snow geese heading south for winter. A few rapid blinks of the eye, and we're helping them pack their rooms for college or marriage.

Sadly, many men fail to appreciate the children-in-the-home era until it's gone. Some fathers, in fact, do all they can to escape the ruckus. The daily effort it takes men to stay in their zoos and tend to their monkeys can feel exhausting. Fatherhood is a never-ending job. Reed Markham said, "Being a great father is like shaving. No matter how good you shaved today, you have to do it again tomorrow."

This is why many men take a pass. They leave the parenting role to the wife and retreat to the office, woodshop, or golf course. Arguably, it's more fun to chase a golf ball around a freshly cut fairway than to chase kids.

It might be more fun, but I've seen the pain and regret that this absence from fatherhood creates in a man's heart. A few years ago, Darrel walked into our church and asked to speak with me. His eyes were bloodshot, and his hands were shaking as he slumped into the chair by my desk. Walking into a church and sitting in a pastor's office made him noticeably uncomfortable. He picked a spot on the carpet between his boots and stared at it the entire visit.

The first thing out of Darrel's mouth was "Pastor, my kids hate me. They live here in town, but they won't even talk to me. I can't take it, so I drink every night to escape the pain."

I met with Darrel several times over the next few months. Each experience was the same as the last. He'd come in smelling like booze, find a spot on the carpet to stare at, and then tell me about how trips with buddies and extra hours at work had taken precedence over family vacations, school programs, and his children's baseball or soccer games.

The last time we met, Darrel said, "I don't blame my kids for hating me. I don't like me much, either."

There was little I could do for this man in his sixties. But he did quite a bit for me. I learn a great deal from counseling others. My time with Darrel impressed upon me the idea that to live without regrets, I'd better stay engaged in my zoo. No matter how noisy or out of control my monkeys get, I must see every day as a chance to make positive memories with my kids.

There's a song that plays through my mind several times a week. I hear this tune in my head when I'm wrestling, fishing, or reading to my children. It's Pierce Pettis's gem "You're Gonna Need This Memory."

With a great melody, Pettis encourages men to pay attention to the memory that, right then and there, is in the making. He sings, "I've seen baby hands reach out, grab my fingers like a vise, grab my glasses, grab my keys, grab my heart by the strings. Hold on, boy, you're gonna need this memory."

Four years ago, when Aidan was three, Jamie and I took all three kids fishing on our boat in a sand-pit lake. It was a warm, breezy night early in the summer. Pillowy cotton drifted down from the trees and coated the pond like a layer of snow. Ours was the only boat on the water. The children ate pretzels, dipped their fingers in the water, and found dinosaurs and turtles and other shapes in the clouds.

I kept busy baiting hooks and untangling line. Outdoor outings with three children younger than seven don't last long. After about an hour, Claire was throwing rocks into the water, and Kate, like her mom, had turned to a book to pass the time. Even Aidan had stopped fishing to play with the shiny red and white bobbers in his Spider-Man tackle box.

I was just about to turn the boat toward the dock when I noticed we had a small chunk of a worm left in the Styrofoam cup. I persuaded Aidan to put down his bobbers and try one more cast. We threaded the chubby abdomen over the hook and flung it fifteen feet from the boat. Within two seconds, it was bouncing up and down.

"Hey, buddy, you've got a bite."

Aidan's eyes were about as big as the baby sunfish I could see pecking at his chunk of worm.

"Hold on, bud, don't jerk yet . . . I'll tell you when." Finally, the little fish sucked in the bait, and I yelled, "OK, now!"

It took all the strength in Aidan's tiny arms to reel in that five-ounce fish, but he hung in there.

As the sunfish flopped around in the water by the edge of the boat, something astonishing happened. What we saw hushed everyone on the boat (for the first time all night). A huge form emerged from the depths of the pond. At first, I thought it must be a branch that had dislodged from the bottom and was floating to the surface. As it got closer and closer, it looked less like a branch and more like a largemouth bass. The largest bass I'd ever seen in all my years of fishing.

The next few moments were a blur. The bass slammed Aidan's sunfish with its mouth open so wide it could have swallowed a softball.

I grabbed the net, and with a lucky dip of the wrist, I brought both fish into the boat and onto the floor in front of four sets of stunned eyes. From nose to tip of the tail, the fish measured twenty-three and a half inches. Our family celebrated that moment as if we'd found the lost city of Atlantis.

I have a photo of Aidan struggling to lift the fish up off the ground. He's smiling so hard his eyes are pinched shut. When I snapped that photo, I could hear Pettis singing, "Hold on, boy, you're gonna need this memory."

I could have fished alone that night. It had been a stressful, people-intensive day at the office. When I clocked out at five, I'd planned to get away by myself. But at the last minute, Jamie asked, "Would you rather have company on the boat tonight?"

I shudder when I think of the memory that almost wasn't created.

THE MOST IMPORTANT QUARTER

A man may get seventy, perhaps eighty years on this earth before his last sunset. The time that our children live under our roof, needing us to wrestle, tickle, discipline, snuggle, bait hooks, and do the hundred other things dads are designed to do lasts eighteen, perhaps twenty-three years. That's about a quarter of a man's life.

This is the most important quarter. Yet it's also one of the busiest. These children-in-the-home years tend to occur at the same time that men are establishing their careers. Their success at work often provides additional income to spend on hobbies and recreational activities. Work, hobbies, and sports are fine pursuits, but not if they replace the time our kids need us to spend in our zoos.

Life has a way of getting busy and then getting away from us. It's a part of the human condition. I've probably heard the voices of two hundred older fathers tell me, "Make the most of these years when your children are at home. They go by quickly." I believe these voices. They haunt me as I push my daughters on our rope swing out back or as I teach my son how to hold his glove when he's catching a pop fly.

When I drive my youngest child to college, help her move

in, and then hug her good-bye, I want to drive away exhausted. Spent. Tired not from the move but from the past twenty-seven years of giving my children every ounce of everything I had to offer as a dad. I can't imagine the regret of saying good-bye to those in-the-home years while realizing that there was so much more that I could have done.

There's a poignant moment at the end of the movie *Schindler's List* that I think about when I think about saying good-bye to the in-the-home years. Oskar Schindler is being honored and appreciated by a crowd of Jewish men, women, and children whom he helped save during World War II. Itzhak Stern, Schindler's accountant and friend, hands him a ring, which has written on it in Hebrew, "Whoever saves one life saves the world entire."

Schindler breaks down in tears. For all he did to save people, all he can think about is how he could have done more.

Schindler replies to Stern's gift by stating, "I could have got more out. I could have got more. I don't know. If I'd just . . . I could have got more." A moment later, Schindler looks at his car with despair in his eyes. "This car. Goeth would have bought this car. Why did I keep the car? Ten people right there. Ten people. Ten more people."

As Schindler drives away, the streets are lined with the faces of the people he saved. Their eyes are reflective and thankful. But his eyes are sullen, filled with grief. He's battling his demons. He could have done more.

I don't want to drop my youngest off at college or walk her to the front of the church and feel that I could have done more. I want to feel utterly exhausted and completely satisfied inside.

THE EXHAUSTED, SATISFIED FATHER

Fatherhood is complex. Men wear many hats and play many roles. But as I've watched excellent fathers make the most of their parenting, I've noticed two strong themes: teaching and cheering.

TEACHING

When it comes to learning how to live well, schools aren't the primary educators of our children. Sunday-school teachers don't carry that burden. Friends and peer groups certainly play a role, but they don't take the lead, either. Fathers and mothers are the most important influence in a child's life.

In Deuteronomy 6:7, parents are commanded to "teach [the words of God] diligently to your children, and . . . talk of them when you sit in your house, and when you walk by the way, and when you lie down, and when you rise."

That passage paints a picture of active, intentional parenting. Fathers can't just hug their kids in the morning before school and then play a little catch with them in the evenings; the picture of fatherhood presented in the Bible requires much more intentionality, time, and effort. Fathers help their children learn how to live well. That takes time, a lot of time.

Broadly defined, living well involves knowing God and responding to Him appropriately. It also involves relating to other people in loving and appropriate ways. Nobody is born with the wisdom to know how to live well. That wisdom is taught. It's picked up through observation, through asking questions, through following the examples of others. Deuteronomy 6 presents a picture of one generation learning to live well from the one before it.

That being said, it doesn't always work this way. Loving, godly fathers have children who grow up to make poor choices. Alcoholic, drug-addicted fathers have children who grow up to be good, honest men. Parenting isn't a formula that if performed well produces a perfect child.

Good parents don't parent for a *product*. Their primary goal as parents isn't to produce godly children. Their primary goal is to be faithful to God. Goals ought to be something we are in control of to a certain extent, something we can achieve. The hearts of our children are in God's hands, out of our control. What isn't out of our control is how we choose to use our time every day. A faithful father will choose to teach and model a life lived well, in dozens of ways each day.

One of my clearest examples of a *teaching* father is Larry, a pastor and friend from Iowa. Larry and I worked together for four years, taking several trips out of town for ministry. At the end of our day of ministry or conference messages, we'd call our wives and children. Larry's son was in his preteenage years, and his daughter was a couple of years older. As I overheard Larry talking with his wife and children, I began to discover the secret of being present, without physically being in the home. He would speak gently to his children, asking them questions about their day. He'd talk about his day with them, repeating his thoughts, feelings, and lessons that he had learned in the conference. When his children handed the phone to their mother, Larry would talk to his wife in a slightly different, even gentler tone of voice.

When Larry's not on the road, he's an actively engaged father. He knows Deuteronomy 6, and he seeks to teach his children through the organic, everyday activities of life. He holds their hands as he prays before dinner. He rubs their heads when he prays with them at night before bed. He gets to know their friends. He's always looking for natural ways to discuss truth and relationship with them as they go through their days together.

Teaching our children takes time, a lot of time. Teaching takes intentional togetherness. Much of a father's teaching happens in the house, at the dinner table, or while tucking children into bed at night. Men have a tremendous opportunity to show their children how to live well while enjoying their favorite interests, especially when that interest involves the outdoors. One of the best ways a dad can teach and demonstrate his affection is by taking his kids into the most sensational classroom in the world, the great outdoors. Few things expand and deepen a child's heart and view of the world more quickly than experiencing nature with a thoughtful, instructive parent.

When I was young, time outside with my mother or father put life in perspective. All of the petty, miserable politics of the grade-school playground or the junior-high lunch room disappeared for me when I was outdoors. One of my most vivid memories is from third grade. A group of fifth-graders made it their goal to see how long a sentence they could stream together with words that rhymed with *Zeke*. There are a lot of words that rhyme with *Zeke*. I still have the final product locked in my memory: "*Zeke* the *freak* is a *geek* who took a *leak* in the *creek* for a *week*."

Looking back, I can appreciate these fifth-graders' ingenuity. But in that moment at recess, when that final sentence was thrown at me with prideful precision, it placed a wet blanket over my entire existence. You might say Zeke felt *bleak*. I walked home, hating my name and doubting whether my future held any hope or potential for positive experiences.

When I got home, I went fishing with my mom for three hours beneath the mill outside town. The sound of the water rushing over the blades of the turbine, the smell of fresh air, and the feeling that we were all alone under the big blue sky took me home with a sense that everything was right and good in the world. We talked about why some people put other people down. We talked about how to respond to people who aren't kind. We talked about how to choose friends carefully. We talked about how important family is in protecting us from the difficulties of the world. That time outdoors helped me calm down and feel more hopeful about my future.

The outdoors is already helping me build relationships with my kids. When I take my three monkeys fishing or on a hike in the mountains, nature gives us serene, undistracted moments to ask questions and talk through answers. Two weeks ago, my daughter Kate needed a turkey feather in order to make a quill pen for a school project. So, on my day off, I drove Kate to the woods, and we tromped around outside for two hours, looking for shed antlers, identifying tracks, and searching for turkey feathers. She talked nonstop. She asked questions about why God created creatures as weird as turkeys, how her mother and I met and fell in love, and why I chose to become a pastor.

"Hold on, boy, you're gonna need this memory."

Aidan can't quite talk as much or as fast as Kate. But a few months ago, I took him into the timber near our house to help me hang tree stands, and he talked my ears off. When I attached a stand in a cottonwood by the river, Aidan threw rocks into the water and told me about the dozen things he wants to be when he grows up. Later, as we rode the four-wheeler through the forest, he sat between my legs and told me who his best friends are and what he likes about them. A while later, when we stopped on a trail to identify deer tracks, he listed all the reasons he's thankful that I'm his dad. When we returned home, he raced on ahead of me, burst through the door, and yelled in the deepest voice he could summon, "Mom, I did a bunch of cool stuff with Dad today!"

Psychological research shows that there are three primary things adults remember fondly when they grow up: family meals, family vacations, and time spent outdoors. My mom, who's in her sixties, wrote a book about her childhood. In this book, she reflected on a moment outdoors with her dad: "My one luminous memory of my father is of a night in 1955 we spent together in Port Isabel, Texas." She wrote: "One night Dad and I went fishing alone on a wooden dock. As I watched him cast and reel, I savored the warm air, the crash of the sea and the briny smell of the water." My mother wrote about that memory:

> I felt happy, safe and hyperaware of what I was experiencing. I wanted to remember my father humming and pulling in fish, my nubby, striped jumper, white T-shirt and bare feet on the splintery dock. I wanted to forever hold in my heart and mind the silvery moonlight, the tartness of the orange soda and the staccato red lights of the fishing boats rocking in the water. Such peace and joy with my father were rare and significant.[1]

Teaching our children how to live well doesn't happen in bursts. It's not something that we schedule to do at intermittent intervals. If Deuteronomy 6 shows us anything, it paints the picture that one generation passes on wisdom to the next, and the next, through the daily and weekly routines of life. This is why it's so important for men to take their children with them at times when they chase a pursuit. Being present with their kids, whether on a golf course, in the woodshop, or on the deck of boat, provides the time and place fathers need to teach their children how to live well in this chaotic world.

One of the ways fathers teach their children is through discipline. Good fathering doesn't consist of merely setting rules and enforcing them, but a father who loves his children will teach them that consequences follow poor choices. When children are young, this process usually requires some form of discipline, as Proverbs 13:24 teaches: "Whoever spares the rod hates his son, but he who loves him is diligent to discipline him."

The point of that proverb is that an active, committed father will understand that his children don't come programmed with the right desires and behaviors. Children need fathers to teach and model what is good and right, and they need fathers who will show them that when we don't do what is good and right, bad things happen. There are consequences. Whether he uses time-outs or other creative means, a father who makes parenting a passionate pursuit will help protect his children and teach them right from wrong through the difficult but vital process of discipline.

CHEERING

One of the best gifts that a father can give his children is the sense that he is *for them*. There's nothing more empowering and comforting than knowing your dad is your biggest fan.

This message is communicated to our children in simple ways, primarily through spending time together. As we'll examine in chapter 11, there's no substitute for large quantities of undistracted time. In a sense, this takes the pressure off us as fathers. Being a loving father is not primarily about saying the perfect thing. It's not about scheduling the most exciting outing. It's not about buying thoughtful gifts or making the fastest Pinewood Derby car. To give our children a deep, empowering sense of our commitment, we must spend time with them.

A friend of mine, Bryan, is a loving father who is for his children. He has three daughters, and one of his highest priorities during the in-the-home years was to make sure that his girls knew that he adored them. Bryan showed his daughters love and support in a variety of ways. He took them on dates. He attended their activities. He tucked them into bed each night, prayed with them, and told them over and over again how proud he was of each of them, and why. Each of his daughters knows precisely what he admires and respects about her. He's told them hundreds of times.

Repetition communicates affection. Bryan formed traditions with his daughters so that they would know how much they mattered to him. For example, every Christmas, Bryan scheduled a one-on-one date with each daughter. He would take them Christmas shopping for the other members in the family. Sometime around November, he'd approach each daughter, ask her on a date, and then write it on the calendar.

Over lunch a couple of weeks ago, Bryan told me, "By the time my girls left the house, I wanted them to know that their dad deeply loved and admired each of them in specific, personal ways. I wanted to send them into the world having locked into their souls a deep sense that they are loved. I wanted to liberate them to be who they wanted to be."

Children never forget fathers who have cheered them on.

That positive, loving influence sticks with the child long after the father is no longer present. In Nathan Miller's book *Theodore Roosevelt: A Life,* Miller describes Roosevelt's father's role in his son's life: "No one had a greater influence upon his namesake. By example and instruction, he imbued Theodore, Jr., with a strong sense of moral values and remained an almost palpable presence at his side long after his death at the age of forty-six."[2]

Fathers who cheer their children on remain by their children's side when they get into the world and form their own families.

Likewise, fathers who don't cheer, who don't prove that they are *for* their children, also remain a palpable presence in their children's lives. But not in a way that is productive or encouraging.

A friend of mine, Joseph, reminded me of this reality. His dad didn't cheer him on—quite the opposite. And I'll never forget how I learned about his story. It was during an elk-hunting trip a couple of summers ago. Joseph and I were driving between two hunting spots. We'd hunted hard all morning, hiking up and down mountains, bugling into canyons, and glassing hills and valleys. Mid-morning, we decided to grab some drinks and drive to a new area. We pulled in to a gas station to buy a couple of sodas, and when we got back into the vehicle, Joseph did something odd; he shook up his thirty-two-ounce bottle of Mountain Dew and twisted the cap ever so slightly to let the carbonation escape. He repeated this process three more times—shaking, twisting, and releasing the carbonation. When the Mountain Dew was flat, he removed the cap and took a big swig.

I was completely baffled. I thought people drank soda because of the carbonation. I asked Joseph for an explanation.

He replied, "You can thank my ol' man for how I drink pop today."

He explained that when he was a child, his father would take him and his older brother on trips. At the beginning of the trip, his dad would buy each of the boys a two-liter of Mountain Dew and tell them that they had to make it last for the entire journey. Joseph's dad and older brother would finish their two-liters quickly. Joseph drank his as fast as he could but couldn't quite keep up.

As soon as Joseph's dad finished his soda, he'd reach into the backseat and take hits off of Joseph's bottle.

Joseph's tone of voice was resentful as he told me this story. He said, "He never asked. He never apologized. He just kept drinking my pop."

One day, Joseph figured out how to hold on to his Dew. If he'd shake it up, let the carbonation out, and make it go flat, his dad didn't want it. Joseph learned to love flat pop. Joseph told me, "To this day, I can't drink Mountain Dew without making it go flat first."

Both Theodore Roosevelt and my friend carried a strong sense of their fathers' presence, yet in very different ways. Roosevelt said about his dad, "My father . . . was the best man I ever knew."[3] After telling me the tale of how Joseph learned to drink Mountain Dew, Joseph said about his dad, "My father was a selfish jerk."

ZOOKEEPING

Dads, our monkeys need us. We can paper-clip our noses, if necessary. We can stuff some cotton into our ears. We can stand on our porches and take long, deep breaths before opening the front door and entering our zoos. That's fine. Whatever it takes to enter our homes and stay engaged as fathers is worth doing. Whatever it takes to see the race to its end and know that we spent everything we had to spend as fathers on our children is worth it.

Zookeeping is a passionate pursuit we'll never regret.

I wanna have friends that I can trust,
that love me for the man I've
become not the man I was.
I wanna have friends that will let me be
all alone when being alone is all that I need.
I wanna fit in to the perfect space,
feel natural and safe in a volatile place.

—THE AVETT BROTHERS, "THE PERFECT SPACE"

Luke alone is with me.

—PAUL THE APOSTLE, AT THE END OF HIS LIFE

9

STRONG, TALL CEDARS

When I was a child, my dad said something poignant about friendship. Thirty years later, it still defines the subject for me.

I was eight years old, and we were playing catch with a baseball behind our house. I was in a curious mood, and I asked him several questions about his childhood, his parents, and what it was like to grow up in a small town in rural Nebraska.

When we reached the topic of friendship, my dad said, "When it comes to loyal friends, Randy's at the top of the list. If I called him and said, 'Randy, I can't tell you why, but I need you to cut your arm off and mail it to me,' he'd reply, 'Which arm, Jim?'"

What an image to give an eight-year-old boy.

I've spent the past three decades looking for saw-ready friends like Randy.

I've found a few, and I think of them as my shelterbelt. When you live in Nebraska, you appreciate the value of shelterbelts. In the winter, the freezing winds from the Dakotas encounter little resistance as they sweep south across the plains. If it weren't for strong, tall cedars, being outside from December through February would be unbearable.

I went bow-hunting last December, on the coldest day of the year. The wind chill was negative 50 degrees. I put on every piece of warm clothing I had in my closet. I looked like the Michelin Tire Man dressed in camouflage pants and coat.

I drove to the farm and parked the car by the barn, two hundred yards from the tree line. The wind slapping my cheeks stung like pellets from a BB gun. I was in serious pain by the time I reached that first stretch of cedars in the Platte River shelterbelt. That walk across the open field had about knocked the life out of me. It also caused me to panic. As I neared the trees, I pulled my cell phone out of my pack to call the landowner and ask him to pick me up.

I'd just found his phone number by the time I reached the tree line. But as I was getting ready to push the call button, I realized that I wasn't cold anymore, at least not desperately cold. The wind was gone. I'd made it twenty-five feet inside the shelterbelt, and it was quiet and calm. The strong, tall cedars had locked branches to form a wall of protection from the elements. I rubbed my hands together for a moment, warmed up, and then hunted for three hours before making the journey back to the car.

Shelterbelts protect us. They defend us from forces that might otherwise do us in. That's also what loyal, trusted friends do for one another.

Two years ago, I experienced nine months of depression. I was in unfamiliar territory, struggling to figure out what was wrong with me. I've always had more than enough energy for work and play. I wake up with my feet on the floor, ready to charge into the morning. But from September through May, I could barely generate sufficient motivation to get out of bed. I'd lie on my back, staring up at the ceiling for twenty or thirty minutes, searching for a thought or feeling, something that provided enough motivation to sit up, take a shower, and get going.

My family and friends are the ones who enabled me to survive those nine months. They locked branches and formed an impervious wall for me. They gave me space when I needed it. They ran to my side when I needed it. They listened well and gave very little advice.

One friend, Brett, called me once a week, just to leave his voice on my answering machine. He knew that I didn't have the energy to answer my phone, so he expected to leave a message when he called. Yet he dialed my number over and over again, just to fill my voice mail up with messages that he was thinking about and praying for me.

When my depression passed, I began answering my phone again. One of the calls I received was from Brett. He was, in turn, experiencing a depression of his own. He knew that I could understand and would know what he needed. I did, and it was a privilege to be there for him. That's what strong, tall cedars do for one another. They protect and shelter so that life doesn't do them in.

That's not all they do, though. Life is filled with more than just difficult moments; it's brimming over with exciting, vibrant moments, too. These same friends not only make the bad moments tolerable, they make the good moments richer. As Thomas Jefferson said, "Friendship is precious, not only in the shade, but in the sunshine of life; and thanks to a benevolent arrangement of things, the greater part of life is sunshine."

When I think back to my moments of brightest sunshine, it's the people who stand out in my memories. Like the time I climbed Mike's Mountain in Baja, California, with three college buddies. We woke up early and had the mountain to ourselves. A hundred yards up, we took off all our clothes, except our hiking boots and socks, and conquered that cliff au naturel. I don't know why we did that. For that matter, I don't why I'm telling you about it. But that's one of my favorite memories, and it was my scantily clad friends who made that moment thrilling.

Another one of my favorite memories is from the time our small group booked a retreat center in the mountains of Big Bear, California. We pulled out of life for three days and ate olives, bread, and cheesecake as dense as the marble island in the kitchen of the lodge. We played games, listened to music, and had long conversations. That was one of the best weekends of my life, and it was the people who made it special.

Another one of my finest memories is from the time Jamie and I went to Beijing with four close friends. We were so eager to experience Chinese culture that as soon as we touched down in Beijing, we drove straight to a Chinese opera house. Jet lag set in the moment we sank down in the thick, padded theater seats. For three hours, the six of us sat in the middle of the room, heads bobbing up and down to the discordant Chinese music. To this day, we can't talk about that memory without laughing so hard our eyes pinch shut.

I am a man rich in poignant memories, some difficult, some exhilarating. The clearest images in these memories are of the friends who were with me.

AMBITION AND FRIENDSHIP

Friendship is especially important for men who tend to go overboard. Ambitious men need trusted friends to step into their lives, point out potential pitfalls, and help them get back on track. This is in part because men who take risks and chase hard after their passions tend to get knocked down more frequently.

When I was in junior high, my baseball coach would pitch to us in practice. He could bring the heat, but the ball rarely crossed the plate in the strike zone. Most of the time, it soared overhead, skipped off the dirt, or smacked the batter. We never knew what we'd get when we stepped into the box.

Some of my teammates stood in the back of the box, legs bent like coils, ready to spring forward or backward to escape a wild pitch. This is how some men approach life: cautious, reserved, hoping to avoid the wild experiences. That's never been me. I've never stood in the back of the box. When I faced my coach, even though I was nervous, I'd grit my teeth, crowd the plate, and lean toward the mound as he completed his windup. I wanted to hit the ball back at him so hard that he'd have to duck to get out of its way.

Like my coach, life throws wild pitches. It's unpredictable. It comes at us fast and furious. Aggressive, pursuit-driven men who crowd the plate tend to get hit by more pitches. When you take more risks, put your heart and shoulder into your pursuits, you tend to experience more pain and loss. Some is a result of taking risks and trying new things. Some is the result of poor choices.

When zealous men cross lines and get into trouble, it's often their closest friends who help them recognize it. Friends help friends beat addictions to alcohol, gambling, and pornography. Men help their friends out of financial messes. Friends help friends let go of lesser commitments in order to fulfill greater ones. Sometimes a strong, tall cedar can be even more effective than a spouse at helping a man choose the best for his life and then live it.

One of my friends from California told me about how a close friend pulled him back from a dangerous path. Scott was given a heritage of strength. His father was a career Marine and a college football player. His grandfather was a World War II prisoner of war. To be a man in Scott's family was to be made of steel. When I first met Scott in 1999, he was a policeman in the inner city of Los Angeles. In 2010, when he told me this story, he was serving as a fireman and a paramedic.

As do the men in his family before him, Scott appreciates strength. So, when Scott's son, Matthew, was born with several physical problems, it challenged Scott on a deep, personal level. For the first few years, Matthew's life was one asthma attack and emergency-room visit after another. To Scott, these were all signs of weakness, and weakness in his family couldn't be tolerated.

Scott told me, "As his father, I believed my primary role was to toughen him up. It was deeper than a belief, though. It was an instinct that came from someplace way down deep. I needed to make my kid into a man."

Scott said, "So, when Matthew fell down and scraped his knee, I told him to get up, stop crying, and brush it off. If he got sick, I told him it was in his head. I loved my son very much but felt a weird type of embarrassment when I saw him do something weak."

Scott's good friend Kevin had watched Scott and Matthew interact on several occasions. One day, Kevin watched Scott push his son to be strong, and Kevin spoke up.

Scott described the moment like this: "I'd met Kevin for coffee and had taken Matthew with me. Matthew ran around the table while Kevin and I chatted. At some point, Matthew fell down and started crying. I felt my chest tighten. I felt my face flush with embarrassment, or shame, or something. All I know is that I had to toughen him up. I stood up and said sternly, 'Matthew, get up. You're fine. Stop crying.' As I finished the last sentence, I felt a strong hand grip my shoulder and turn me around. Kevin was inches away from my face, looking me in the eyes.

"He said to me, 'Scott, you're going to lose your son if you keep this up. I don't know what's going on inside you, but you've got to chill out. He's just a kid.'"

Kevin's rebuke landed like a slap on Scott's face. It was painful, but it sobered Scott and made him look deep inside himself in order to understand what was causing him to try to parent the vulnerability out of his son.

Scott saw a counselor for a year. He explored the legacy of strength he had been given. He came to terms with his insecurities that drove him to present an appearance of strength. Because of Kevin's rebuke and the counseling that followed, Scott better understands himself, his family, and, most important, how to be a loving and encouraging father to Matthew. Scott told me, "How do you thank a friend like Kevin? Because of him, I'm able to love my son for exactly who God made him to be."

BEST MEN POSSIBLE

My closest friends and I have hunted in Alaska, fished in Canada, and hiked mountains in Romania, Kazakhstan, and Mexico. We've roofed houses, trained dogs, and worked side-by-side on our houses and farms. We've chased a lot of dreams together. Yet the greatest pursuit that my closest friends and I chase together is helping one another become the best men possible.

Men will have varying definitions of what it means to be "the best men possible." For me, it means trying to honor God with my life. It means being a faithful husband, father, and friend. It also means that I work hard in my positions as a pastor and a writer but balance my hours so that I don't make my other relationships sacrifice more than they ought.

My friends know the goals I've set for my life. They also know that I count on them to help keep me on course. In order to help them help me, I've given them permission to ask personal questions about how I'm doing in my marriage, parenting, and other commitments. I've even given them permission to ask me questions about my inner life, my thoughts, and feelings. That probably sounds risky and a bit invasive. It is. But as a group of guys who are trying to be the best men we can possibly be, we've found that risk and invasion of privacy are necessary at times.

FRIENDSHIP OVER COUNSELING

It's been my experience that in many instances, a shelterbelt of friends can be far more helpful and directive than hours and hours of psychotherapy. At times, I certainly recommend people to counselors. Some issues are so deep and pathological that men need a good counselor on their team. Yet I've seen many men turn their lives around and become good, solid men because they've sought out and developed strong friendships.

Men's groups, Bible studies, accountability relationships—small groups of friends meeting to discuss life and the Scriptures—have helped thousands of men talk things out, discuss values, and plan changes. It's been my experience that therapy, as it happens in a sterile "therapeutic" setting, is of limited value to men. David Wexler, a clinical psychologist and author, identified three reasons that men are averse to seeing a psychologist:

> Men often resist standard therapy because they have a hard time admitting that anything is wrong or, if they think something is wrong, they struggle to identify what it is. Another reason they avoid therapy is that they can't tolerate the internalized stigma—the felt shame—associated with feeling needy, dependent, or incompetent. A third disincentive, even with men who know they need help, is the very idea of sitting in a room, talking out loud about all this touchy-feely stuff; it creeps them out.[1]

Men who struggle with opening up and expressing themselves in a counseling office often reveal their secrets to friends. I've been in men's groups where men cried with one another about loss, encouraged one another to rise above an addiction, and walked with one another through the great and the horrible moments of life. I've watched men rise out of a period of inactivity and visionless living and begin to chase a new picture for how their lives can be. That's the power of men connecting with men, as Proverbs 27:9 affirms: "Oil and perfume make the heart glad, and the sweetness of a friend comes from his earnest counsel."

A DIFFICULT WORK

Finding strong, tall cedars and developing them into a life-giving shelterbelt is not an easy work. In Nebraska, cedar trees are everywhere. Sometimes they develop where you want them. Most of the time, they're just in the way. Give a patch of exposed ground enough time, and a shelterbelt of cedars will grow *accidentally*.

It's not so with friendships. It's been my experience that men have a hard time growing and maintaining healthy relationships with other men. There seem to be a couple of challenges that consistently spring up in men's relationships.

COMPETITION

Ambitious men are often competitive, and this can be a good thing. There's nothing wrong with competition for the love of the game. However, competitive feelings often work against friendships. If love involves putting other people first, then the drive to outcompete a friend is a competing value. It's impossible to serve, cheer on, and support someone you're trying to beat.

As discussed in chapter 5, unhealthy competition finds its roots in Genesis 3. When people lost their sense of perfect significance and meaning in God, they searched for it in themselves. When self-worth began to be sought after through performance, performance needed to be measured. How do you measure performance? You have to compare yourself with other people. Then, to feel good about yourself, you must come out on top. Whether it's in a career, a sport, or a hobby, men who live by the Performance Story will always struggle with friend-ships. They will struggle to love other men well, because other men are simply people to outperform in order to feel valuable. Even friends are rivals.

The man who lives in the Grace Story, however, will be able to love his friends well. When a man understands that he fully measures up and is significant because of the grace of God, he will not need to compare or compete. Friends don't need to be rivals; they can be people the man of grace supports and cheers on. This is precisely what Paul describes in Galatians 5:13: "For you were called to freedom, brothers. Only do not use your freedom as an opportunity for the flesh, but through love serve one another." The Grace Story is the only narrative for life that enables people to love perfectly.

The man who "must win at any cost" is typically a man trying to increase his sense of self-worth and contentment by beating others. This type of competition is the great killer of companionship. It also just smells really, really bad. Last summer, I received a phone call from a sportsman that left that smell circling my nostrils. I didn't know Greg well, so I was pleasantly surprised by his call. My first thought was, *This is great. Greg's reaching out, wanting to strike up a friendship.*

All Greg did on the phone was tell me about his accom-plishments. For thirty minutes, I was Greg's audience. He told me story after story of the incredible archery shots he'd made on large game animals. I'd occasionally try to interject a story of my own, but he'd interrupt me with his slightly bigger, more exciting version of my experience.

I'd rather have been sitting in a dentist's chair for thirty minutes than on the other end of that phone call. Greg was ambitious and successful, and I can appreciate that. I'm usually drawn to enthusiastic people. But his inability to get outside himself and celebrate someone else's accomplishments kept the conversation from feeling mutual. Men must learn to be other-centered and genuinely interested in other men's lives. Men must be living by grace to have the fullness a friendship can provide.

COMMUNICATION

Communication is often the second great obstacle to building shelterbelts. Whether they say too much or don't say enough, men often struggle with words. An idiotic sentence nearly destroyed one of my friendships a few years ago.

Jake and I had been close friends for fifteen years. I did something that bothered him, and he talked to our mutual friend, Sam, about it. When I heard that Jake had talked with Sam, it bothered me. The three of us sat down to work things out. At one point during that conversation, I said something along the lines of "Jake, if you aren't willing to be a good friend to me, I'm sure that there are other guys who'd like to take your spot."

I know. What a childish, immature thing to say, huh? If you could only see me blush with shame as I type that quote. I handled conflict in first grade better than I did in that moment with Jake.

Jake is one of my closest friends. I've met few people who have been more loyal to me. In spite of my thoughtless comment, I'm deeply committed to him and our friendship. My statement, however, made Jake feel expendable. He heard me say that I was capable of throwing our friendship away, without having it affect me deeply. What a foolish miscommunication.

In his pain, Jake pulled away from me. Like someone who breathes on a mirror and watches his breath slowly dissipate, our friendship disappeared over the next two years. I was oblivious to my comment, so I was confused and hurt, too. Finally, two years later, our mutual friend, Sam, told me how I'd hurt Jake. I felt sick. I called Jake and asked for his forgiveness. He gave it to me.

I tell that story because it's an example of how easily one insensitive comment can take a chainsaw to the base of a strong, tall cedar.

Incidentally, not enough of the right words can be equally lethal. While it's true that my comment nearly destroyed our friendship, Jake's silence almost nailed the coffin shut. If Jake had told me how I'd hurt him right away, I would have asked for forgiveness much sooner. If Sam hadn't stepped in, Jake and I might have lost a relationship that had been vital for both of us.

It's been my experience that zealous, ambitious men who run hard after their pursuits tend to make mistakes with their words. Like choosing a bit too much club for a golf shot or running over another player on the way to the hoop, we tend to use our words a bit too aggressively.

Because we wound, and are wounded, easily, one vital

strategy toward keeping friendships healthy is to clear the air from time to time. As with a dusty old house at the end of a long, dry winter, it's good to open up the windows and let the wind blow through. The spring-cleaning question that I've used quite a bit over the years is "Have I done anything to let you down or hurt you in any way?" Often the answer is no. However, I have also had friends share an offense with me. I've had the chance to ask for forgiveness and set things right because I asked that question and my friends answered honestly.

Competition and communication are two of the largest challenges to building and keeping long-lasting friendships. But there are more. Many more. Establishing a shelterbelt of friends is not an easy work. But once it's in place, it's life-producing. Committed, solid friendships are worth every ounce of effort we're willing give them.

MEN WITHOUT WORDS

We've already talked some about words. Words poorly spoken. Words chosen perfectly and delivered with encouragement. Words are vital to deep friendships. Yet sometimes men don't need words. We don't always need to speak to be strong, tall cedars. Sometimes we just need to be present.

Women sometimes have a hard time understanding that men can have intimacy and feel supported without talking. Comedian Brian Regan made fun of the difference between how men and women relate with their friends. In his stand-up act, he shared a story about his wife's astonishment at his lack of communication with his friend. Brian had just spent five hours golfing with his recently divorced best friend, and he didn't ask his friend if he was seeing anyone. Regan shared the dialogue he had with his wife:

Wife: How's Gary?

Brian: I don't know.

Wife: Oh, I thought you were going golfing with Gary today.

Brian: Well, I did.

Wife: And you don't know how he's doing?

Brian: It never really came up. Did you ask me to ask him that?

Wife: No, I thought maybe you'd think to ask him that.

Brian: I didn't think of that.

Wife: Well, is he dating anyone?

Brian: I don't know . . . how would I know something like that?

Wife: Were you two in the same golf cart?

Brian: Yeah.

Wife: You're kidding me. You were in the same golf cart for four hours and you don't know if he's dating anyone?

Brian: (awkward pause) . . . I know he's got a new driver.

That dialogue illustrates the age-old difference between the male and the female brain when it comes to relationships.

Sometimes what men need most from a friend is his presence. They want a companion, someone to swing a club with. Just because men don't talk about their feelings doesn't necessarily mean that they're not being supportive. Friends have hundreds of ways of communicating that they care about one another.

Scott Swain, a sociologist, describes men's communication style as a "covert intimacy."[2] Men may not wear their emotions on their sleeves, but they still find dozens of ways to express their care and concern. When my wife and I left for seminary in California, I said good-bye to three of my closest friends. When we came home at Christmas break, this group of friends planned a special meal on our behalf. When we arrived at the party, the three guys were nowhere to be seen. When I walked through the kitchen and into the family room, they jumped out from their hiding spots and dog-piled me. They held me down for about three minutes, pinching and poking me in the ribs and legs. I had bruises on my body for about two weeks.

I'd never felt so loved in my life.

Some of the strongest expressions of love that men give and receive from one another come from a punch in the arm, a slap on the rear, or, in the case of my friends that Christmas, a fairly aggressive dog pile. "Covert intimacy" is not necessarily shallower than expressing intimacy through emotive language. Intimacy is about communicating commitment and support, and many men can do this very successfully without words.

Author Henri Nouwen once wrote: "We probably have wondered in our many lonesome moments if there is one corner in this competitive, demanding world where it is safe to be released, to expose ourselves to someone else, and to give unconditionally. It might be small and hidden. But if this corner exists, it calls for a search through the complexities of our human relationships in order to find it."[3]

I've spent the past three decades looking for that safe, supportive corner in life. I've found it in my strong, tall cedars. You can, too, if you're willing to do the work and make the commitment.

I am not myself by myself. Community, not the highly vaunted individualism of our culture, is the setting in which Christ is at play.

—EUGENE PETERSON,
CHRIST PLAYS IN TEN THOUSAND PLACES

10

THE DAMNABLY DIFFICULT
ADVENTURE

Over the last twenty years, there are few things that have irritated, stretched, and exhausted me more than my interactions with the local church. As a part of this "church," I'm soberly aware that I've been the same irritating, stretching, exhausting force for others, too. Living in spiritual community with others is often a frustrating endeavor. Eugene Peterson described it perfectly: "Getting saved is easy; becoming a community is difficult—damnably difficult."[1]

Things just get weird within the walls of a church. People with various backgrounds, theological views, and strong opinions bring expectations into the church that they wouldn't dare take into any other arena in life. In what other environment would you find judgments flowing so freely on topics such as drinking alcohol, spending money, or even how people dress? Yet those issues, and many more, are on the table when people stand in the foyer of their local church.

I've had a parishioner complain to me that another parishioner's lawn looks junky. I've heard several people disapprove about how other church members have spent too much money on vehicles, houses, and jewelry. I even had one man visit my office to inform me of a most offensive transgression: a Sunday-school teacher in our church had a wine rack in her kitchen. He stated, "Pastor, that's just not right. Perhaps you should stop by her house and tell her that she's crossed the line."

Um, yeah. I don't think so.

Living in spiritual community is treacherous terrain, and many men call it quits. When we look at the void of male commitment in the American church, it's easy to draw the conclusion that men aren't interested in spiritual things. It's been my experience, however, that this is far from true. Just because men are absent on Sunday morning doesn't mean that they are unspiritual. Most of the men I know do think deeply about God and their inner lives. They just don't want to do it in a church with other churchgoers. They'd rather do it through a rugged, individualistic brand of spirituality that is increasingly popular today.

I spoke at a sportsmen's event in upstate New York last winter. As three hundred men filed through the doors and loaded up their plates with wild game dishes, the pastor of the host church told me that he'd never before seen many of the men. After my talk, a line formed by the stage. I shook hands and met about fifty men. I was curious about the pastor's statement, so I asked many of the men where they went to church. At least a dozen men told me that they'd given up on church a long time ago. One man told me, "I quit attending years ago, once I realized that church is full of hypocrites. Now my sanctuary is the great outdoors."

Many men love to pack up their hiking boots, sleeping bags, and pocket Bibles and flock to men's retreats in rugged settings. Men enjoy books like *Wild at Heart* by John Eldredge or *The Measure of a Man* by Gene Getz, while sitting beside a mountain stream or resting beneath the sturdy trunk of a California redwood. On any given Sunday, men with beards, buddies, and Bibles explore the wild places of our beautiful nation. These are deeply spiritual men.

Spending time alone or with small groups in wild places is important. I try to schedule regular personal retreats every year. There are few things that feed my spirit more than leaving my razor, computer, and organizer at home to spend several days with God in the mountains or at a remote retreat center. We all need time away in rough and rugged places.

Yet if that's the only, or primary, way that we connect with God, we're missing out on one of the most challenging adventures God's designed for us: the challenge of community.

THE GREATEST CHALLENGE

When we throw up our hands and walk away from the church, we walk away from the most central, dynamic work that God is doing in the world. It's easy to miss this reality. It's one thing to sense God's active presence when we're in nature. The serenity and vastness of a wilderness area cause us to sigh and say, "God, you are *here*." There is a natural sense of the divine that we find when we center our lives around God while breathing in the fresh smell of pine needles and listening to the roar of a mountain stream.

It's not necessarily quite so easy to stand in wonder and worship when we're surrounded by dozens of people who have bugged us one too many times. However, according to Scripture, God's work of pulling imperfect people together for the purpose of worship is His most mysterious, powerful, primary work in the world today.

God is in the business of drawing people together. His central design has always involved pulling undeserving, flawed, sinful people together for the purpose of worship and community. Forests are inspiring. Mountains and valleys are invigorating. The oceans and rivers that rush and roar across the face of our planet are breathtaking. But all of these beautiful places exist to serve God's greater purpose of forming a people after His own heart. Nature isn't the terminal goal. Community is, and if community is one of God's main objectives, it makes a man's choice to separate from the church seem foolish.

Men were made to make a contribution. For a Christian man to live the fullness of life that Jesus promised in John 10:10, he must choose to relate deeply with other Christians. As Eugene Peterson writes, "There can be no maturity in the spiritual life, no obedience in following Jesus, no wholeness in the Christian life apart from an immersion and embrace of community. I am not myself by myself. Community, not the highly vaunted individualism of our culture, is the setting in which Christ is at play."[2]

MEN OUT OF CONTROL

Passionate, pursuit-driven men tend to be control freaks. In order to rise to the top of their careers, hobbies, or sports, they need to understand and control as many variables as possible. The men who best understand and control the process are the ones who often achieve greatness.

Being in control of certain things isn't bad or wrong. However, for a soul to form fully and well, he must find himself *out of control*, at times. He must come to grips with the reality that he isn't the master of his destiny, the orchestrator of all people and events occurring around him. A sense of smallness is vital to a sense of wholeness.

This is one of the reasons that immersion into a community is crucial. No man can control a local church. Spiritual community is a messy, untamable, living organism that continually reminds him that he's not in charge.

Our family is part of a rural, multigenerational, growing local church in the middle of Nebraska. As much as I appreciate our church, there are several things that I'd like to see changed, much of which has to do with style or "flavor" issues. But I've also got opinions about how people should treat others differently. I've got strong opinions about the ministries that I'd like to see improve or expand. I'm one idealistic, opinionated person in a church of about three hundred idealistic, opinionated people.

Even as the lead pastor, I have a limited ability to change things at our church. This is especially true in the most important arena, the heart. When it comes to the hearts of the people at Heartland EFC, I have *no* power to effect change. That's God's work.

Not a week goes by that I don't see the muddy, messy activities of a church filled with sinful people, myself included. Not a week goes by that I don't come face-to-face with my inability to purify myself and other people and make things look the way I'd like them to look. Not a week goes by that I don't try to make large, sweeping changes. In my five years at Heartland, I've dealt with stalkers, gossips, and child abusers. I've helped a spouse file a police report against her husband. I've tried to talk a dozen couples out of divorce. I've counseled girls who are cutting themselves, men addicted to pornography, and adults who were dealing with depression. I've seen a great deal of pain and hurt, and I've done what I can to fix people and make our church healthy.

After five years, I'm utterly convinced that our church, like all churches, is too messy and mysterious for any one person to control. All people have mud stuck to them. The more people, the more mud. The more we interact, the more we get one another and everything else we touch muddy. Someone who likes things to be nice and neat, according to his expectations, often finds church extremely challenging.

By now, you might be thinking, *I thought he was trying to persuade me to make a commitment to my local church.*

That's exactly what I'm doing.

If they want a deep and mature soul, aggressive, intelligent, and accomplished men need to feel small and powerless sometimes. It's taken me twenty years to *begin* to appreciate this reality, but church—the good, the bad, and the frustrating—has made me more aware of God, other people, and my need for grace. Men must feel vulnerable and powerless sometimes in order to grow. Nothing has brought this sense to me more accurately than my experience with my local church.

The local church's ability to humble a person reminds me of spending time in nature. Standing beside overwhelmingly powerful forces, such as Niagara Falls or the Grand Canyon, makes me feel small and out of control.

I'll never forget the time Jamie and I visited the Cliffs of Moher in Ireland. My grandfather's family on my mother's side came from Bray, Ireland. They crossed the Atlantic and landed in the Americas to escape the potato famine. I had always wanted to visit Bray and explore my roots. Jamie and I rented a car in Dublin and spent a week working our way south and west along the coastline. We ate dinner every night in a pub and then spent the night in the most idyllic bed-and-breakfast we could find in the area.

When we reached County Clare along the western shoreline, we visited the Cliffs of Moher. Why there aren't railings along those cliffs, I have no idea. The landing we stood on rose seven hundred feet above the Atlantic Ocean. From that height, the breakers looked like tiny fingernail clippings. It took me ten minutes to summon the courage to get on my belly, slither to the edge, and peek over. Even then, I made sure Jamie had a good grip on the heel of my shoe.

I lay on my stomach looking over that cliff for about five minutes. Those were deeply contemplative minutes. I felt small and insignificant in comparison with my surroundings. Not only were the cliffs enormous, but it was a clear day, and I could peer across hundreds of miles of ocean. Lying on that smooth strip of shale, I felt tiny, insignificant. Any feelings of self-importance I had when we'd parked our rental car were gone the instant I peered over the edge.

I drove away from that moment transformed. After five minutes of looking over the cliff along the Atlantic Ocean, I looked at my life differently. It's hard to feel masterful when you're in the presence of something so enormous. When I carefully slinked back from the edge, stood up, and walked away, I retained the sense that I was a small, expendable part of something so much greater than myself.

Phillip Brooks said, "The true way to be humble is not to stoop until you are smaller than yourself, but to stand at your real height against some higher nature that will show you what the real smallness of your greatness is." That's what the Cliffs of Moher did in me: they showed me my smallness.

We consider our church in Central City, Nebraska, as a hospital. Each of the pastors has a doctor's coat hanging on a hook to remind us that we're helping hurting people. For some reason, Heartland seems to attract wounded, abused, and pained people. We also draw people who have been disillusioned by past experiences with the church. On any particular Sunday morning, we might have three hundred adults walk through our doors. That's three hundred different sets of pain, expectations, and worldviews roaming our halls.

There's no way that I can fully understand three hundred different souls, let alone control them and turn them into what I want them to look like. Most of the time, I do not feel masterful as a pastor.

Aggressive, pursuit-driven men don't like to feel powerless. They'd just give up and move on to an area of life that they are able to affect and improve. In our area of Nebraska, on any given Sunday morning, you'd hear the shotgun blasts from dozens of duck hunters along the Platte River. You'd see a handful of men golfing at the country club just south of town. You'd find men in overalls working on tractors in the dozens of large red barns that dot our county.

Hunting ducks, golfing, fixing tractors—these are activities men can control. They can influence and steer the outcomes. Hardworking, forward-thinking men often flee church to participate in activities that make them feel powerful and in control. I've felt this desire. I've spent a handful of evenings, over the course of these past five years, viewing job listings in careers *outside of the church.*

Twenty years ago, I'm ashamed and amused to confess, I

entered a local church feeling full of myself. I walked through the foyer doors, into the sanctuary, and thought to myself, *These people have no idea how fortunate they are to have me with them today.*

Ridiculous, I know. As I was thinking those thoughts, God was no doubt looking at me and thinking, *I've got so much work ahead of me with this fellow.*

That was twenty years ago, and I still feel prideful too much of the time. But I've glimpsed true humility and strength. I've known several dynamic, strong, but humble men who were in the final stages of life. Their years in the church have given them a different attitude. They have a sense that they're the ones fortunate to have the church. One older parishioner told me, "I have no idea why the church has put up with me all these years. But I'm so glad she did."

I'm not that humble yet. But I'm also not at the same place I was when I became a Christian and brought my boulder-size ego through the sanctuary doors that first Sunday morning.

God is responsible for this slow and steady development of my character, and He's used other people in the church to make these changes in me.

THE TRULY GREAT FRONTIER

It's important for men to be honest about what frustrates them about church. But church is more than sitting in a building feeling disappointed. So much more. There's no greater opportunity for men to rise and live out true masculinity than within their local community of faith. Two clear and powerful images have emerged as I've watched men interact with local churches:

men are given countless opportunities to take care of others, and these same men are cared for by others.

Other-centeredness is one of the great virtues in life. True masculinity involves subordinating our safety, comfort, desires, and needs to help someone else. For example, we have about a dozen single mothers in our church. Last year, Rick, a twenty-eight-year-old man, abandoned his wife, Shelly. Rick told his friends that he just got bored with his life. He moved out in October, leaving Shelly to care for their five-year-old son, Shawn.

At the time Rick left, Shelly only had a part-time job. It was impossible for her to keep the house, feed her son, and pay the bills. She listed the house with a realtor and signed a lease for an apartment in town.

I watched about ten truly great and masculine men from our church respond. They mowed Shelly's lawn, helped clean and repair her house before it went on the market, and even took Shawn out for ice cream while Shelly visited the courthouse for custody hearings.

These men acted like kings. Servant kings. Warriors. They remind me of Aragorn from J.R.R. Tolkien's *Lord of the Rings*. At end of the last book, *The Return of the King*, Aragorn is crowned the king of Gondor, the most powerful country in the world. That is a spectacular moment, made even more spectacular by how that king had spent his life rescuing hobbits, women, and other creatures and countries. Aragorn consistently subordinated his safety, comfort, desires, and needs to do good to others.

The men in my church reminded me of Aragorn in those months following Shelly's divorce. Without being asked, they swooped in and took care of two vulnerable, hurting, desperate people. Shelly and Shawn still go to our church today. They're genuinely happy, well-adjusted, well-cared-for people. They were carried through the past year on the backs of strong, zealous men who spent less time fishing, golfing, and working on their own lives in order to meet someone else's needs.

That display of masculinity had an impact on Rick. I played basketball with him a couple of months after he left his wife and son. After the pickup game, he came up to me and said, "Zeke, I've never seen anything like what the men in your church have done for Shelly and Shawn. Why did those guys do all that?"

I replied as gently as I could, "That's what men do, Rick."

In my church, there are a thousand stories of good men meeting other people's needs. Warrior kings sweeping in and rescuing people. The church provided these men with opportunities to be great, needed. However, it also gave these men something else—the opportunity to be taken care of. We all need to be taken care of sometimes.

I was reminded of this a couple of weeks ago as I helped John, a leader in our church, bury his wife. Laura had a disease that caused her to die slowly, gradually declining in her ability to speak and care for herself. When John wasn't working, he attended to his wife's every need, making dinner, helping her in and out of the bathroom, and cleaning the house. But John had to work full-time in order to maintain his health benefits, so he wasn't able to be by Laura's side during the daytime.

Eight women from our church helped John every day during those final six months. They arrived before he left for work and stayed for a while after he returned home. They prepared meals and placed them in his freezer. They cleaned his house. They took Laura to doctor appointments and to visit friends.

John and Laura had been active participants in our community for about twelve years. They'd prepared meals for others during times of need. They'd played on our Sunday-morning worship team. They'd started ministries in the church. They'd planted themselves deeply into spiritual community. Their investment came back to them a hundredfold. When they went through the most difficult crisis they'd ever faced as a couple, a community of friends walked them through it. The local church caring for its men is the second strong, inspiring image that I've witnessed in the church over the past twenty years.

MORE THAN SUNDAY

Church is what we do on Sunday mornings; this is one of the largest misunderstandings a man can have of spiritual community. Our best study of the Bible and its context reveals that Christians in an area or town interact as a large family. They hold their worship services in homes. They participate in one another's baptisms, weddings, and funerals. When someone is sick, the other believers show up to pray and meet needs. Early Christian believers lived their lives together. Worship services in the early church were not isolated, pristine spiritual events. They were extensions of organic relationships lived day in, day out.

Church can offer incredible things to men, but men need to invest themselves fully. Stepping into the church from time to time doesn't work.

I had a man approach me in a hardware store once and tell me, "Pastor, I've watched people reach out and help Jack [another man in our church] when he lost his job." Then he asked, "I lost my job, too. How come nobody helped me?"

I had to ask this man his name before answering him. His face was vaguely familiar. I'd seen him a couple of times at our church but not enough to know anything about him. I told him that I was sorry that he didn't feel supported. I encouraged him to come to church on Sunday and said that I'd help him connect with a couple of people who could maybe help.

He replied, "Yeah, I don't know. Church really isn't my thing."

It's on our shoulders to make a deep commitment to a local church. Then it's on our shoulders to stay put, through the good and the bad.

There certainly are reasons at times to leave a church. But, in my opinion, there aren't many. People are imperfect and messy. They are hypocrites. They do have annoying personality traits and habits. People get on my nerves and let me down all the time.

But I'm no prize, either. I'm painfully aware that my personality doesn't bless people with one delightful experience after another.

Most of our differences and frustrations can be worked through and transcended, if we make deep, abiding commitments. Far too many people enter and exit church without having ever made such a commitment. When we immerse ourselves in a local church, over time, our spiritual community helps us become our best selves.

OUR BEST SELVES

After Adam and Eve disobeyed God in the garden, God cursed them. The curse is spread far and wide, across the skies, land, and sea. It has altered man's relationship to the environment. The curse has also crept in like an infection to sicken the terrain of our marriages and our relationships with our children, friends, and neighbors.

But as dark as the curse is, the brightness of Christ is brighter still. And one of the ways that God shines Christ into our lives and lifts us out of the darkness is through our brothers and sisters in Christ who love us the most. There's a fascinating phrase in Paul's letter to the Ephesians. We find it in chapter 4, the section that describes God's plan for the church. Paul describes the role that our community plays in our spiritual development: "*truthing* in love, we are to grow up in every way into him who is the head, into Christ." Many translators have rendered that verse as "speaking the truth in love," but the word in Greek is simply the verb form of *truth*, or *truthing*. One of God's key strategies for our spiritual growth involves you and me truthing each other in love.

This verse presents the picture of a church family growing closer to God as they pursue truth together. Listening for truth on Sunday mornings that they can apply to their lives together. Speaking the words of God to one another throughout the week. Living out the truth together in their homes, their workplaces, and the public square. Sometimes truthing in love involves speaking. Sometimes it involves doing. Often it involves simply being together. God often does powerful things in our lives when we spend time with people who walk in truth.

Like many other people, I can get caught up in defeating thoughts about who I am and who I'm not. My deficiencies and sins. The pain others experience. The complexity of life. These thoughts and worries can all send me to a dark, bleak place where negative thoughts race through my mind a thousand miles a second. I'll hear defeating, demanding voices in my head at night. Sometimes all day long. This is a difficult world to live in. We all suffer.

A few weeks ago, I was feeling discouraged about the ministry, my parenting, and my friendships. When I met a friend for a burger, my spirits were low.

Then we talked. We warmed up. We started on one subject, then another. We laughed, talked about the grace of God, and found ourselves celebrating our families. For two hours, we simply enjoyed each other's company. And God was there.

Those two hours lifted me out of the darkness I'd been in when I walked into the restaurant. Bryan's presence and spiritual friendship took me from a place I could barely tolerate to a place I wanted to stay in.

Experiences like this are hard to explain. I can make several statements that would touch on what happened. Bryan helped me stop believing lies I'd believed. He helped me see who I really am in Christ. He took my focus off the defeating thoughts racing through my mind and put them onto the truth about the great things in my life. He didn't necessarily mean to do these things. But this is what time spent with the body of Christ can do.

We were not fashioned to survive this world and its offerings as lonely individuals. God desires to be a light for men, a force that outshines the darkness of sin and death. He does this largely through His body, the church, as we pursue truth together.

To recognize the best things in life and find the energy to pursue them with passion, we need one another. We need spiritual community. We need to be *truthed* by people who love us and love God. We simply aren't ourselves, our *best* selves, without others.

Here dies another day
During which I have had eyes, ears, hands
And the great world round me;
And with tomorrow begins another.
Why am I allowed two?

—G. K. CHESTERTON

How we spend our days is, of course,
how we spend our lives.

—ANNIE DILLARD

11

FULLY HERE NOW

During a pheasant hunt last season, a friend told me a story that made us both cry. While we were resting in the cab of his truck, sipping hot coffee before walking the next field, Mike asked how my book was coming along. When I told him that I was working on a chapter on men spending time with the people they love, he sighed and said, "Unfortunately, I've got a story for you."

Mike had grown up in a poor family in Omaha. Mike was a hardworking, industrious man. When he was in his mid-thirties, he took a large risk and purchased a small company in Grand Island, Nebraska. The risk paid off. Three years later, he owned one of the fastest-growing, largest-grossing companies in the Midwest.

Mike loved his wife and kids and understood what his priorities should be. However, during those first few years of success, he spent about seventy hours a week at the office. When he was at home, he'd be working in his home office. His wife and four children sensed that they came in second place.

Mike justified his absence from his family with the idea that a man's primary responsibility is to provide for them. When he was young, his parents couldn't afford to buy him new shoes or pay for camp. He was now able to meet not only his family's needs but also their every whim and want. In his mind, he was doing well as a husband and father.

Mike explained how this misconception came crashing down with one statement from his son.

"When Greg was twelve, all he wanted to do was play baseball. He always had a glove on one hand and a ball in the other. When I came home from work, he'd be pitching baseballs through a tire out back or hitting them into the field. I got home late every night from work. It was almost dark when I pulled into the driveway, too late to play catch." Mike swallowed hard again as he said, "I couldn't seem to get home earlier. Work was just *the* priority."

"One night, after brushing my son off, I went into my office, sat down at my desk, and felt guilty. Then I thought of the perfect solution. I went online and ordered hundreds of dollars of baseball training equipment and videos. Within two weeks, my son had enough baseball gear to make a college team jealous. He had a batting cage, bases, throwing nets, and all sorts of strengthening devices. As I clicked the 'place order' tab on the Web site, I felt like a good dad again. I'd made it possible for my son to play baseball from the time he got home from school until he went to bed."

Greg played with that gear for one week, maybe two, and then completely lost interest. In fact, he seemed to lose interest in baseball altogether. For a month, that equipment sat in the shed. When Mike arrived home from work, Greg would be playing video games or watching television.

Mike told me, "Every night, I got more and more upset. Finally, I came home one night from work, and Greg was on the couch watching TV. I just lost it. I yelled, 'Greg, get up and come with me! I marched him outside, opened the door to the shed, and pointed at all that gear. 'Do you know how much this equipment cost me? And you haven't touched it in weeks. I thought you wanted to play baseball?'"

Mike swallowed hard and wiped tears from both cheeks.

"While I laid into him, Greg stood there with his hands in his pocket, looking down at the floor. When I finished, he was quiet for a few moments. Then, without looking up at me, he said, 'Dad, all I ever wanted to do was play catch with *you*.'"

Mike had grossly miscalculated. For his son, it wasn't about becoming good at baseball. It wasn't about learning how to hit a home run or turn a double play. It wasn't about expensive training equipment. It was about spending time with his father.

Mike's error is a common one in the world of ambitious men. He underestimated the value of being present.

There's no substitute for men being present with the people they love. Physically present. Eyeball to eyeball. Shoulder to shoulder. There's no piece of baseball equipment in the world, no matter how expensive, that can replace that experience.

Dallas Willard writes, "The natural condition of life for human beings is one of reciprocal rootedness in others. As firmness of footing is a condition for walking and secure movement, so assurance of others being for us is the condition of stable, healthy living."[1]

This sense of rootedness in one another develops in large part from spending time together. Most of the time, the activity or setting doesn't matter. I took my nine-year-old daughter with me to run errands last Saturday afternoon. We went to the hardware store for a new tire for our mower, then to the gas station, and then we stopped by the John Deere dealership to pick up a couple of new wheel clamps. When we got home, Kate jumped from the truck, hugged me, and exclaimed, "That was so much fun, Daddy!"

We didn't go for ice cream or to the water park. We went to a hardware store, a gas station, and a tractor dealership. But it was the sense of loving companionship that gave Kate a great afternoon with her dad.

ABSENT WHILE PRESENT

Presence is important, but it is possible to be bodily present without being emotionally present with one another. This seems to be a particular challenge for energetic, hard-charging men. It also seems to be a particular challenge today in light of the amount of distractions that offer to carry us away from the people who are with us.

Men today face a challenge that their grandfathers didn't face. We're constantly introduced to new technology that promises to make life easier. Laptops, smartphones, and digital readers are all marketed as devices that simplify life so we can enjoy more time with the people we love.

That might be how those products are marketed, but it's not necessarily what they're doing. The real appeal of these devices is that they keep us from experiencing the passing of time. Time is a funny thing. We tend to enjoy it when we're not conscious of it. Prison is said to be "serving time." "Time just flew by" is a phrase often used to describe pleasurable moments. If there's one thing that active, zealous men cannot stand, it's time moving slowly. When we're checking e-mail, Facebook, or our favorite blogs, we're not feeling that intolerable boredom. So we purchase products to beep, chirp, and chime loud enough that we can't hear the clock ticking.

This escape from boredom can be a dangerous, almost addictive experience. Today's generation of men are growing up hyper-stimulated, buzzed on video games and devices. There's nothing wrong with cell phones or computers. However, when our relationship with these devices keeps us from slowing down, unplugging, and enjoying long, calm moments with the people we love, they have damaged that which they promised to save: our time.

I coached my seven-year-old son's coach-pitch baseball team this summer. During the last game of the season, I slipped out of the dugout and walked to the bleachers to get a bottle of water. There were about a dozen dads sitting in the stands, the majority of whom were texting or searching the Internet on their smartphones. When I stepped back onto the mound to pitch to our team, I noticed that several kids had to get their dads' attention before stepping up to the plate. They wanted to make sure that their dads had their phones down and were watching them bat. I watched one of the players, in his little white baseball pants and an oversized batting helmet, hit the backstop with the bat a couple of times to get his dad to look up.

Long gone are the days of dads actually watching their sons' baseball games. Where did they go? Perhaps smartphones, being so smart, could tell us.

It's one of the great ironies of our era; we have more time-saving devices than at any other point in history. In five minutes, I can pay a month's worth of bills online, print out directions for our family vacation, and find out the cost of gas in every major city between our house and Los Angeles. Astonishing.

Yet one of the most common complaints I hear from men is that they don't have enough time to spend with their families. Wives and children echo this complaint. One of the most common comments I'm hearing from the families of ambitious men is that their husbands and dads don't spend enough time with them. When they are around, they're staring at a phone, computer, or television.

Does technology really help us accomplish the greatest priorities in life? My grandfather, Bernard Thomas Pipher, didn't have a cell phone hanging from his hip. He was a lawyer who filed all of his papers by hand. When he wanted to look up a phone number or an address, he used one of those strange, archaic woody devices called phone books. If he needed to submit a document to the courthouse, he didn't hit a send button. As crazy at it may sound, he walked to the courthouse, up a long flight of stairs, and handed the document to the clerk.

Was Grandpa Bernie's life more difficult? Perhaps in some ways. I'm sure he got an occasional paper cut from the phone book. I'm sure his legs got tired walking to and from the courthouse several times a day. I'm sure that his pre-time-saving-device life was at times inconvenient.

Yet my grandfather always had time for me. Time to take me for an ice-cream cone or to help me ride a bike or to take me to the swimming pool. My most dominant memories of him involve sitting and talking. Sometimes we'd be in the kitchen. Sometimes we'd be at the café. Sometimes we'd be in the car. Wherever we were together, I had his undivided, undistracted attention. I never had to snap my fingers or tap him on the arm until he looked me in the eyes. He was always already watching.

We need to be physically present with one another. But that's not enough. The people we're with need to know that they have our full attention. This requires unplugging, powering down, and leaving the cell phone on the counter at times. It requires sitting in the front row of the bleachers and cheering, without being begged. It's not enough to be at the ball field. We've got to be present in the game.

A PARTICULAR CHALLENGE

As men advance in their careers, taking on more leadership and responsibility, they often become more efficient. Accomplished men learn to lead and relate to others *from a distance.* We send memos, draft policies, and place other people in charge.

This economizing isn't necessarily a problem or a vice. In fact, for many men to be successful and help their company advance, they need to hand things off and put others in charge. Men often need to lead from a distance. Efficiency builds companies and creates jobs.

Edward Cecil Guinness is a good example of this reality. Edward's great-grandfather, Arthur Guinness, was the founder of the caramel-colored Irish lager.

Guinness beer did well under the first three generations of Guinness leadership. But it wasn't until the fourth-generation visionary leadership of Edward Cecil Guinness that the company exploded with wealth and success. Much of the new success can be attributed to Edward Cecil's leadership style. Where his father, grandfather, and great-grandfather had spent much of their time and energy with their employees and community, Edward delegated. He hired competent, driven people and then delegated a great amount of leadership to them. He led from a distance. Stephen Mansfield described Edward's leadership style in his book *The Search for God and Guinness*. He writes, "Though he would lead the company to new heights, he would do so through delegating authority to exceedingly capable men. It was a management style fit for the age."[2]

Hundreds of decent-paying jobs were created during an economically difficult period. Dublin, which had been a sick, disease-infested village, turned into a thriving, industrialized city. Mansfield writes, "Edward Cecil Guinness put £250,000 into the hands of three trustees to create the Guinness Trust, 'to be held by them in trust for the creation of dwellings for the labouring poor' in Dublin and London."[3]

Thousands of people benefited under Edward Guinness's relational and leadership style. Edward's story is one example of how it can be a good thing when zealous, aggressive, enthusiastic men lead others from a distance in the workplace.

Yet this relational style rarely produces good things at home. It's impossible to be connected to our loved ones *from a distance*.

God designed families to experience personal, deeply intimate relationships. Husbands need to know their wives' hopes, fears, and feelings. Fathers should be experts at snuggling, reading books, and pretending to lose in wrestling. A man who is connected with his family will know how to run a waffle iron, do underdogs on a swing set, and hug and kiss his wife in front of his children. Happy families are connected families.

This design for connectedness springs from the very nature of God. As a triune being, God experiences this mutual, life-giving, intimate relationship as one divine being with three distinct personalities.

This triune nature of God is certainly one of the most mysterious aspects of His being. Triune means that God, while being one essence, consists of three distinct persons. These three persons make up the one, unified godhead.

The Bible describes this relational nature of God in several places. For example, in the very first chapter of the Bible, we're introduced to a God who exists in relationship with Himself. In Genesis 1:26, we read that God said, "Let us make man in our image, after our likeness." We know from Genesis 1:27 that God wasn't speaking to the angels. He wasn't speaking to some other created being. God was speaking to Himself yet referring to Himself with the term "us," because He, by nature, is a relationship.

God is relational, which means that His perfect happiness and pleasure is based in part on a profound, mysterious connection among the three distinct persons. God is infinitely satisfied, and it is a *relational* satisfaction.

The pleasure that the triune God experiences relationally has profound implications for how men will find the deepest pleasure and satisfaction in life. People have been made in the image of God, which means that we will find our deepest satisfaction when we are relationally connected to our family. Men who lead from a distance at home will struggle. They will struggle with their relationships. They will struggle with their consciences. They will struggle with living out one of the most essential, basic aspects of their relational nature.

The relational nature of God is a deep and mysterious doctrine. I can read about it, think about it, and talk about it until my brain hurts. Yet, in some sense, the relational nature of God in us is simple. It's easy to understand and appreciate. We experience it when we are enjoying the rightness of relationships well lived. We see it when the others around us relate deeply with those they love.

I saw a man live out his relational nature and purpose this

summer at the swimming pool. It was the middle of July, one of those days that make you loathe summer and long for the cool, low-humidity days of fall. It was ninety-four degrees at six o'clock, so Jamie and I took the kids to the water park for the last two hours of the day. Jamie and I wanted to sit in the shade, drink iced coffee, and talk about our day. The kids wanted to do flips and spins in cool, clear water.

While we sat and talked, I watched a father carry out the relational image of God in him with his three boys and his wife. For an hour, he went off the boards with his three sons. He'd do flips, dives, and cannonballs. After he swam to the side, he'd grab the ladder and watch as his three children tried to mimic what he'd done. He watched every jump or dive they made, and then, when their little heads popped up out of the water, he celebrated as if they'd just won the Olympics. Those three boys never had to say from the diving board, "Dad, watch this!" They already sensed that he was watching.

After an hour or so, this father and his sons moved into the shallow water and did somersaults. Then, a bit later, they held races. They'd start in the middle of the pool, and their mother would say, "Ready, set, go!" The three kids would splash like mad trying to beat their dad to the wall. He let them barely touch him out every time. The dad surely had pruny fingers; he was with his three children in the pool for two hours. We walked out at the same time as his family, and I watched his three children cling to his side all the way to the car.

This man, like my grandfather, is an attorney in our small town. Unlike my grandfather, I suspect he owns a laptop and a smartphone. But they weren't at the pool with him that night. This man was going to be reciprocally rooted to his wife and children, and nothing was going to stop him.

FULLY HERE NOW

This idea of being present with the people we love can be described in three words: Fully. Here. Now. Men who learn to be fully here now with the people they love will not miss the most important moments in life.

Each of these three words is important in describing how men should spend time with others. *Fully* emphasizes the way in which we're present. To be *fully* present means that when we're with our wives, children, and friends, we're not texting, we're not on the phone, and we're not distracted by the television. To be *fully* present is to direct our eyes, thoughts, and affections entirely toward our companion.

The word *here* locates us in a place. This is not necessarily natural for hyper-hobbied, pursuit-driven men. We like to try to be in as many places as possible. To be *here* means that we're not at the office. We're not on a trip. We're not up in our bedrooms taking naps or tucked away in the garage working on our old cars. We're here, in the physical presence of the person who is with us.

Physical presence is important, but it's not enough. We must also be tuned into other people when we're with them. That's what the word *now* stresses. Ambitious men often struggle with living in the now. They're always thinking of work, hobbies, or their next adventure. They're considering the past and making plans for the future. It's not hard for zealous men to be on a daddy-daughter date and be thinking the entire time about what the rest of the work week will involve.

This ability to think outside the present has its place. This skill is absolutely vital for men who hope to keep up with their responsibilities. But for men to be reciprocally rooted to the people they love, they must be able to stop planning meetings, fishing trips, or house projects and just allow their complete attention to be directed to the present moment in time. It's not enough to be fully here, we must be fully here *now*.

RECOGNIZING A MOMENT

It's impossible for men to be *fully here now* with everyone they love in every moment. Men are an exhaustible resource. They need to work. They need to take trips. They need to leave their children at home and take their wives on dates occasionally. Men have a finite amount of time and attention that they can give to others, which necessarily means that they are faced with dozens of relational decisions each day.

Men will burn themselves out trying to be fully here now with everyone. That can't be the goal. Rather, the goal for men who want to live deep, intimate, successful relationships ought to be to recognize a moment. In any given interaction with another person, men must learn to slow down and appreciate their opportunity to be fully here now.

To recognize a moment means that if we're on a date with our wife, we unplug from our e-mail and texting, and we listen well. We ask good questions. We think about what she is saying instead of what we're going to do at the office tomorrow. If we're playing catch with our son in the backyard, we're asking questions and learning more about the little guy on the other side of the toss. We're not answering the phone or dreaming about the next time we get to mountain climb or geo cache with our friends. If we're with our friends, we're with them in a way that they know we care about them. We may be shooting hoops or walking fields for pheasants, but we're present in a way that lets our buddies know we are there, in the moment, in that place, fully with them.

Being fully here now also involves recognizing *who* is most important to us. A young man on my block learned this lesson the summer following high school. A couple of weeks before graduation, Rodney's parents asked him to leave a bit of time free during graduation weekend. They had invited his grandparents to stay for the weekend, and they wanted the entire family to go out for brunch on Saturday.

Rodney already had plans, and his grandparents weren't in them. He told his parents that all he wanted to do was party with his "good buddies" on Friday night and then not have to worry about getting up and doing anything on Saturday. His grandparents drove six hours to attend the ceremony on Friday night and then drove home the next morning. They were back home in Minnesota by the time Rodney rolled out of bed, stumbled to the medicine cabinet, and took four ibuprofen for his headache.

Rodney left a couple of weeks later for basic training, the first time he'd ever left home. He was gone for two and a half months. He describes those ten weeks as the hardest period of his life. He was lonely, homesick, and always tired. During his time away, not a single friend called. He didn't receive one letter from any of his "good buddies." But he got a letter and a care package every week from his grandparents. Some weeks, it was a box of cookies. Other weeks, it was fresh cinnamon rolls or banana bread. It was enough to feed not only Rodney but also the other twenty-two homesick men in his unit. Every care package came with a letter telling Rodney about home and how much he was missed.

Rodney changed quite a bit that summer. But the change that he talked about with the most passion had to do with who was most important in his life. He said, "I learned who it is that matters most. It's family. I'll never push them aside again."

As Rodney learned, being fully here now involves recognizing the important people in life, those who send cookies and letters during your worst moments, and then choosing to spend your best time and energy on them.

Life gives us many *recognizable* moments a day. You won't have to wait long to practice this skill. I'd guess that as soon as you set this book down, you'll likely find yourself in such a moment that presents a choice. Don't wait for a better one to come along. Seize this one!

This morning, as I was walking out the door for work, my five-year-old daughter, Claire, gave me a chance to be fully here now. My three children are often still sleeping when I grab my keys and turn the knob of the door to leave. They sleep on the second floor, with their doors partly closed and their fans cranking out white noise. Yet most mornings, all three children hear the jingle of my keys as I pick them up. Something about that noise rouses them from sleep and tells them that if they want a hug from Dad, they'd better race downstairs right away.

That's what happened this morning with Claire. She heard my keys jingle, awoke from her deep sleep, then raced downstairs in her flower-patterned footie jammies.

As she walked down the stairs, I was feeling eager to get to the office, make my coffee, and kick off my Monday morning. Still, I also wanted to be fully here now with my half-awake daughter for a moment.

I put out my hands, offering to pick her up, and she fell into them. I lifted her, and her knees slipped into that perfect space between my ribs and my waist. Her little legs wrapped around my back, and she laid her head down on my shoulder. I could feel the warmth from her face that just moments ago had lifted from the pillow. She's the ideal age for a perfect-fit hug.

I recognized the moment and made a simple decision that I'll never regret. I decided that I would hold Claire for as long as she wanted. I wouldn't set her down; she'd have to let me know when our hug was over. If she wanted to stay slumped in my arms for an hour, that'd be fine. I'd just make my coffee an hour later than normal that morning.

We stood in the foyer of our house for about eight minutes. Her breathing was slow and deep, and there were moments when I thought she'd drifted back to sleep. Finally, her older sister came running into the room. She reminded Claire, "Do you know what we get to do today? We're going to the pumpkin patch with friends!"

That was it. Claire began to squirm around in my arms like a bass fighting to jump out of the boat and back into the lake. I put her down and kissed her forehead. She bounded off to begin her adventurous day.

Whether Claire will remember those eight minutes, I can't say. I hope so. I hope that somehow those four hundred and eighty seconds set a sense deep in her heart that her dad adores her. I hope she remembers that moment twenty years down the road. I will. And I hope I'll have thousands more memories to go with it.

Being fully here now creates those memories that make us rich in our old age.

And there's fury in a pheasant's wings.
It tells me the Lord is in His temple.

—RICH MULLINS, "CALLING OUT YOUR NAME"

He would withdraw to desolate places and pray.

—LUKE

12

TOUCH POINTS
WITH THE UNTAMED

A GOD WHO SPEAKS

Life isn't about escaping to the mountains. But the occasional escape to the mountains can infuse men with life.

As I've worked on this book, I've found myself dealing cautiously with the topic of men running to wild, rugged places in search of spirituality. My concern is that too much emphasis on men living individualistic lives, connecting with God only in retreat centers and wilderness areas, can lead to a void in local churches.

However, one of the strong themes of the Bible is that settings *do* matter. God often leads His people outdoors, into rugged, isolated places to accomplish something powerful in their lives.

A WILDERNESS THEOLOGY

The word *wilderness* occurs 266 times in the English Standard Version of the Bible. The word *mountain* shows up 310 times. The word *valley* is mentioned 173 times. Even the word *garden* is used 59 times. Most of the times these four words are used in the Scriptures, they're describing a place where God has led some- one in order to interact with Him in a unique way. These settings aren't necessarily beautiful, idyllic spots such as Niagara Falls or the Rocky Mountain National Forest. In fact, the root word that is often translated as *wilderness* in the New Testament contains a sense of desolation or emptiness.[1] A place doesn't need to be idyl- lic in order to serve as a catalyst of connection to God—wild and desolate places can be perfect settings.

The Old and New Testaments tell several stories of individ- uals interacting with God in untamed places.

Adam and Eve in Eden. Sometimes God *does* place people in breathtaking environments. When He created Adam and Eve, He put them in the most astounding garden imaginable. This wasn't your mom's bean patch behind the house. The Garden of Eden was a utopia of fruits, vegetables, nuts, and wildlife that provided sustenance, entertainment, and companionship every moment of the day. It was in this garden that people learned to relate with their Creator, each other, and the rest of the created world.

Hagar in the wilderness of Beersheba. Hagar, Abraham's second wife, traveled into the wilderness of Beersheba with a child, a bottle of water, and a loaf of bread. God met this outcast there in her lowest moment, immediately after she had placed her son, Ishmael, under a bush to die of dehydra- tion. God is the compassionate provider to the widow and the orphan, and He demonstrated this commitment in this lonely place. He provided a well of water, words of encouragement, and a promise to Hagar that her son would become the father of a great nation.

Israel in the desert of Kadesh-barnea. When Moses led the nation of Israel out of Egyptian captivity, he led them into the desert region of Kadesh-barnea. It was in this arid land that God had the Israelites wander for forty years. *Kadesh* means "holy," and *barnea* means "desert of wandering." God used this dry, isolated land to teach his people numerous lessons about faith and trust.

David in the caves south of Jerusalem. David wrote many of his most introspective, thought-provoking songs while hiding in the caves of Adullam (1 Samuel 22), west of Bethlehem. David fled to these mountainous caves for protection from Saul and his armies.

Nebuchadnezzar in a Babylonian wilderness. When God wanted to reorient Nebuchadnezzar and instill in him a sense of reverence, he sent him to the wilderness. Daniel 4:33 records, "He was driven from among men and ate grass like an ox, and his body was wet with the dew of heaven till his hair grew as long as eagles' feathers, and his nails were like birds' claws." At the end of seven years, Nebuchadnezzar's sanity returned, and the kingdom was restored to him. That time in the wilderness taught Nebuchadnezzar the truth that God "does according to his will among the host of heaven and among the inhabitants of the earth; and none can stay his hand or say to him, 'What have you done?'" (Daniel 4:35).

Namaan in the Jordan River. When God chose to heal the leprous man Namaan, the commander of the armies of Ben-Hadad II, God had him take his head underneath the waters of the Jordan River seven times. God could have healed Namaan with a snap of His fingers. God could have summoned Namaan to the Temple. God could have used incense, chants, and any number of ointments. However, when God wanted to give Namaan health and a sense of the power of God, He sent him to the most famous river in Israel.

John the Baptist in the Judean wilderness. When God called John the Baptist, Jesus's cousin, to inaugurate the ministry of Jesus, he called him out of the cities and villages and into the wilderness of Judea. John ate locusts and wild honey and wore a camel-hair garment. This diet and wardrobe, in that desert location, work together to paint the picture that John wasn't participating in the luxuries of civilization. God sent John to call Israel away from worldly living, and God prepared John for this task in the remote, rugged Judean wilderness.

Jesus in the mountains of Palestine. Even Jesus, God incarnate, pulled away to mountainsides and lakes to pray and spend time listening to His Father. Luke records, "He would withdraw to desolate places and pray" (Luke 5:16). When the crowds pushed in, when the noise became too loud, Jesus pulled away to an isolated place to relate with His Father.

These are just a few examples of how, throughout the Bible, wild, rugged, isolated places provided solitude while being a crucible for relationships. This is still true today. Whether it's a lake, forest, mountain, desert, or prairie, we often hear from God and connect with ourselves while there. The wilderness is also a place where we can bond with other people in powerful ways.

This power in nature should make perfect sense to us. If "the heavens declare the glory of God," as Psalm 19:1 states, then it's only natural that when we're lying outside under the stars, instead of inside under our ceiling fans, we're going to encounter God's glory in a special way. Untamed places offer experiences with God that crowded, paved, manicured environments can't.

So do storms.

A STORM THEOLOGY

I've always been fascinated with storm chasers, men and women who grab their gear and race toward the hornet's nest. I must admit to a hint of jealousy; when a storm rolls in, and I'm holding three children on my lap, a part of me longs to join those thrill-seeking weather junkies who throw on raincoats, grab video cameras, and speed off in the direction of the tornado or thunderstorm.

I'm fascinated with weather. A powerful snowstorm or thunderstorm can turn an otherwise dull day into an event. Our town is situated smack dab in the middle of "Tornado Alley," the region in the United States that experiences the most tornadoes. This fact excites and humbles me.

Just as the Bible presents a theology, or biblical perspective, on wilderness, it also presents a theology on storms. Storms are God's handiwork and often communicate His voice in a unique way. Several times in the Bible, God speaks to people through storms, displays His power through thunder and lightning, or describes Himself as the author and director of what happens in the sky.

The book of Job contains a unique example of God speaking to a man through a storm. Job is a faithful man who had most of his dearest possessions stripped away from him by Satan. Toward the end of the book, Job questions God about the fairness of what God had put him through. Chapters 38 and

39 describe God's reply to Job and are worth reading for the beautiful, poetic language.

But what has always fascinated me about God's reply to Job is that He spoke to this man *through a storm*. Job 38:1 sets the stage for God's address: "Then the Lord answered Job out of the whirlwind."

Whirlwind is the Hebrew word for a tempest or a severe storm. The next seventy verses in Job are some of the most rhetorically powerful words ever recorded. God provides example after example of His perfect knowledge and governance over every aspect of creation. His speech leaves Job covering his mouth and quaking in his sandals, and it all occurs through a storm.

We read about God communicating through storms throughout the Bible. In Psalm 29:3–4, David tells us to view thunder as the voice of God: "The voice of the Lord is over the waters; the God of glory thunders, the Lord, over many waters. The voice of the Lord is powerful; the voice of the Lord is full of majesty."

When God wanted to display His power to Egypt, He threw thunder, hail, and lightning upon the earth. Exodus 9:23 records: "Then Moses stretched forth his rod toward heaven, and the Lord sent thunder and hail, and fire ran down to the earth. And the Lord rained hail upon the land of Egypt."

The New Testament also describes God's communication through storms. Twice in Matthew's Gospel, we read about Jesus working during a storm to teach His followers lessons about faith. In chapter 8, Jesus fell asleep on a boat, in a squall, leaving the twelve disciples to navigate a fierce storm by themselves. Matthew 8:24 records: "And behold, there arose a great storm on the sea, so that the boat was being swamped by the waves."

The disciples were horrified by the power in the storm. They lost sight of who was with them on the boat. They woke Jesus up and cried, "Save us, Lord; we are perishing" (Matthew 8:25).

Jesus woke up, commented on their lack of faith, and then calmed the storm with a command. The disciples responded to Jesus's power over the storm by exclaiming, "What sort of man is this, that even winds and sea obey him?" (Matthew 8:27).

A few chapters later in Matthew's Gospel, Jesus took these same men through another faith-shaping experience in a storm. Once again, a tempest raged against the boat that the disciples were in. This time, Jesus wasn't in the boat; He was walking toward it on the water.

When Peter saw Jesus stepping fearlessly through the squall, he asked Jesus to command him to come to Him. Jesus obliged and invited Peter to join Him. Peter stepped out of the boat and did it. He actually walked on water. Until he saw the storm, felt afraid, and started to sink.

Jesus rescued Peter, challenged him to greater faith, and then the two of them got into the boat. As in chapter 8, when Jesus calmed the storm, the disciples responded with awe. Matthew 14:33 records: "And those in the boat worshiped him, saying, 'Truly you are the Son of God.'"

Two storms. Two encounters with the God who is in control of storms. Two responses of worship and deepened faith.

God has used storms in similarly powerful, personal ways in my life. One moment that I'll never forget happened a couple of years ago during a five-mile jog on the country roads outside of Central City. I left the house knotted up inside, feeling anxious about several ministry situations. Stress attacks my stomach, and on that day, my cramps were so bad that I started my jog hunched over.

Then the storm came. The sky turned from bright yellow to dark grayish-white. Our area of Nebraska is flat. I'm talking *really* flat. There's one hill in our county, and it's three miles away from town. I watched the storm materialize several miles away. By the time I reached the turnaround point, it was almost directly overhead.

The lightning stayed in the clouds, shooting strings of light like a thousand spindly capillaries. A rumble of thunder immediately followed each flash of light. The air felt different, almost electrified.

I've lived around thunderstorms my entire life; I know which kinds are the most dangerous. This wasn't one of the run-for-cover types, so I didn't panic. In fact, I felt more calm and secure than I'd felt all week long.

I made it half of the way home before I realized that the storm was doing something to me. I stopped jogging, sat down by a fence post, and watched the sky change shapes and colors as it blanketed the prairie. For ten minutes, I was reminded of the power and ability of God. When I got up to finish the run, my stomach didn't hurt, and my anxiety about life and ministry was gone. I had encountered God, and like the disciples in the boat, I found that it changed my faith.

TOUCH POINTS

Most men live the majority of their lives surrounded by cars, concrete, and crowds. They go to work someplace inside, often with automatically flushing toilets, drinking fountains, and iridescent lights buzzing above their heads. They live in homes so close to other homes that an overthrown baseball is bound to break a neighbor's window. Their neighborhoods have paved streets and a planned number of trees and are sprayed for mosquitoes in the summer. Most men live in tame environments.

This is pretty much my story. Of the three hundred sixty-five days in a year, I probably spend three hundred thirty of them in fairly unspectacular settings doing relatively mundane things. During a typical week, the green spaces I see mostly involve our family's acreage and the neatly manicured lawns, ball fields, and city parks in Central City, Nebraska.

My typical day involves waking up, making a couple of scrambled eggs or a bagel, and having a cup of dark coffee. I spend a few moments talking with Jamie and our kids before driving the three-mile route to the church where I work. I spend about eight hours at the office studying, writing, counseling, or leading meetings before climbing back into my truck and driving those three miles home. When I get home, I help make dinner, play with the kids, and then write, read, or talk with Jamie for a few hours before going to bed.

Those are the normal rhythms and routines of my life. They take place in normal settings. And if you're still awake after reading those last two paragraphs, I'll tell you that I ardently love my life. I adore my family, find purpose in my work, and have found ways to be creative each day. I also feel very fortunate to live in the place where I live.

There is a sense in which I never want to flee. I refuse to believe the lie that life is what we find when we escape our routines. Life isn't in the escape. It's in the day-in, day-out activities we go through with the people we love. It's primarily enjoyed in the places where we work, fix dinner, and mow our lawns.

Yet.

Yet I do believe that men need the occasional touch point

with the untamed to keep them alive and healthy inside. Moments outside help us experience God's power and glory in ways that are only possible in wild, rugged, perhaps even stormy places. These moments outdoors help to infuse us with life and energy. I believe that they help us hear from God in unique ways.

I've worked hard to encounter God in wild, rugged, isolated places wherever I've lived, even if it involved some travel. For example, I went to seminary in the middle of the L.A. basin, surrounded by cars and concrete. Seminary was grueling. I spent five days a week in class, and most of my evenings studying in the library or a local coffee shop. For three years, I lived among nineteen million other people and their cars, studying Greek, theology, and various aspects of ministry. My brain was always tired. My butt was always chair-sore. My lungs always felt saturated with the poop-colored smog that hovered over the L.A. basin.

God rejuvenated me time and again through frequent trips to San Onofre State Beach. Shortly after moving to California, a classmate gave me an old fiberglass surfboard. Once a month, I'd bungee-cord the board to the luggage rack of our white Ford Escort wagon and make the trek down the 5 freeway to the beach. I'd typically leave early in the morning on a weekday, and I often had the beach to myself. I'd paddle out beyond the breakers and sit on the board facing the ocean. I'd occasionally catch a wave in to shore, but the real thrill was sitting on the board, facing away from the shore, looking at nothing but sky and ocean. A hundred yards from the San Onofre shoreline, facing west, was the only place I could stretch my sight out as far as I could and not encounter evidence of people.

Removing everything man-made from my vision once or twice a month kept me alive inside during those three years.

The ocean gave me a sense of the largeness of God. It made me think of God's power and control. Rarely did I visit the beach that I didn't think about Job 38:8–11:

> *Or who shut in the sea with doors*
> *when it burst out from the womb,*
> *when I made clouds its garment*
> *and thick darkness its swaddling band,*
> *and prescribed limits for it*
> *and set bars and doors,*
> *and said, "Thus far shall you come, and no farther,*
> *and here shall your proud waves be stayed"?*

I rode the Pacific Ocean's proud waves as often as possible. Without those occasional touch points with the sea and the surf, I'm convinced that my studies and my city would have dried my spiritual bones up like grape left out in the summer sun.

Instead, thanks to God and His ocean, when I moved from California to Iowa in a Ford Escort wagon that had surf wax caked onto the luggage carrier, I felt alive and ready for the next phase of life.

THE UNTAMABLE GOD

We have silly debates in church sometimes. In 2004, Christian singer and songwriter Chris Tomlin released an album titled *Arriving*. One of the songs on that album was titled "Indescribable." In that song, Tomlin describes God as being "untamable."

We sang that song in church shortly after its release. Then we argued about it. About a half a dozen people contacted the worship leader to suggest that we shouldn't refer to God as an untamable being. These people felt that that adjective doesn't apply to the Being who created and ordered the universe. *Untamable*, they said, implies something wild, unpredictable, and dangerous. They simply weren't comfortable with those ideas attached to God.

Until this debate, I hadn't thought much about the issue. I decided to study the nature of God and how He works with people. The more I searched the Scriptures, the more I became convinced that God is *the most* untamable person in my life.

When something is untamable, we can't control or subdue it. To be untamable is to be unpredictable, beyond the control or governance of others. God is untamable because He is not a formula. God is untamable because He made Nebuchadnezzar eat grass like a wild beast, turned Job over to Satan, and then became a man who overturned tables, temples, and nations. God is untamable because, as Psalm 115:3 states, "He does all that he pleases."

Most of all, God is untamable because He is a personal being. He has likes and dislikes. He makes choices. He turns left at times when people expect Him to turn right, and He doesn't consult with them before doing it. Singer-songwriter Andrew Peterson celebrates the personal, unpredictable nature of our untamable God in his song "The Reckoning":

> *You are holiness and grace*
> *You are fury and rest*
> *You are anger and love*
> *You curse and You bless*
> *You are mighty and weak*
> *You are silence and song*

You are plain as the day
But You have hidden Your face—
For how long? How long?

God continually surprises us, and because He's God, we can't object. We cannot force God's hand or make Him answer to us. When the Apostle Paul sensed that some people might struggle with God's interactions with humanity, he asked, "But who are you, O man, to answer back to God?" (Romans 9:20).

We simply cannot make God do things our way. He *is* untamable. What's more, I'm convinced that the fact that God is untamable is precisely why people feel close to Him when they're in wild, rugged, untamed places.

PERMISSION TO GO WILD

John Eldredge made a poignant statement about men in his book *Wild at Heart*: "Adventure, with all its requisite danger and wildness, is a deeply spiritual longing written into the soul of man. The masculine heart needs a place where nothing is prefabricated, modular, nonfat, zip lock, franchised, on-line, microwavable. Where there are no deadlines, cell phones, or committee meetings. Where there is room for the soul."[2]

When I first read those words by Eldredge, I felt as if a life-long friend had described me perfectly. That paragraph connected with my soul on a deep level. I've recommended *Wild at Heart* to dozens of men and watched it connect with their souls, too.

However, I've watched several men misapply Eldredge's ideas in hurtful ways, ways that Eldredge would never condone.

A conversation I had with one woman illustrates what some men did with *Wild at Heart*. Sue slammed her husband's copy of the book down onto the desk in front of me and said, "I wish Tom had never read this stupid book!"

She went on to explain that Tom had "found himself" in the pages of *Wild at Heart*. That book, as it had done for me and many other men, helped him understand why he had such a desire to seek adventures in wild places. Then something unfortunate happened. Tom's new and better understanding of himself turned into justification for selfish behavior. When Tom wanted to run off and hike another mountain or golf another famous course, he'd tell Sue, "God made me to be adventurous. It's a part of being a man."

For five years, Tom ran from wilderness area to wilderness area, leaving Sue to take care of the children and the home. She blamed Eldredge's book, which is also unfortunate; nowhere in *Wild at Heart* does Eldredge encourage men to act selfishly toward their wives. In fact, in his chapter "A Beauty to Rescue," he challenges men to put their wives first. Yet the desire for adventure can be strong, as can the heart's tendency to twist good things into selfish passions. Many men found in Eldredge justification to take their "wild" tendencies in selfish directions.

When a man's touch points with the untamed lead him away from his deeper, more vital commitments—his marriage, parenting, work, or friendships—a good thing turns toxic.

PERMISSION TO RUN AWAY

The smell of pine needles, the misty spray from a mountain waterfall, or the sound of cutting through snow on the way down a ski slope will only be soul-deepening, worshipful experiences if men are there *by permission*.

Asking for permission can be a difficult concept for ambitious, accomplished men to grasp. When I spoke with Tom, Sue's husband, I suggested that he should ask his wife for permission before scheduling a hunting or fishing trip. He responded, "Permission? Why would I need her permission? I'm an adult."

Just because we grow up, get married, and start earning an income doesn't mean that we stop needing permission. Healthy, other-centered, mutual relationships are a continual process of asking questions, listening, and surrendering our will to the will of another.

Mike Mason describes mutual submission in his book *The Mystery of Marriage*:

> In marriage it so happens that the Lord has devised a particularly gentle (but no less disciplined and effective) means for helping men and women to humble themselves, to surrender their errant wills. Even the closest of couples will inevitably find themselves engaged in a struggle of wills, for marriage is a wild, audacious attempt at an almost impossible degree of cooperation between two powerful centers of self-assertion. Marriage cannot help being a furnace of conflict, a crucible in which these two wills must be melted down and purified and made to conform. Most people do not realize that this is what they are signing up for when they get married, but this is what invariably faces them.[3]

And as much as hardworking, zealous men need time away in untamed places, they'll only enjoy that time away when they go with their family's blessing. In fact, without permission, or blessing, wild, isolated, rugged places often torment us. They give us time to think and reflect; if we enter these places with guilty, shame-riddled consciences, we end up thinking and reflecting on how we've blown it. There's not a lot of enjoyment in those thoughts and reflections.

It's usually good to ask for permission before rushing out the door with our tents and hiking boots.

But there is an exception. There are times when it's best not to ask our wives for permission. Before all of the women reading this book toss it into the fire, let me explain. I can clearly remember a time during our first year of marriage when asking Jamie for permission was a bad move, an unfair thing to do to my new wife.

I wanted so badly to go with a few friends on a pheasant-hunting trip. But money was tight, and I'd already taken several days off from work to hunt and fish. We were trying to save up our vacation days for a trip together that next summer, so this pheasant hunt threatened our budget and our future plans.

I knew all of these things, and so did Jamie. But I really wanted to go on this hunting trip. I explained how important the trip was and then told Jamie that she could decide. I'll never forget what she said to me.

With frustration in her voice, she replied, "I feel like you're making me be your mother with this decision."

That stung. Let me explain what she meant. We *both* knew the right decision. We both knew that time away would stress our budget, our relationship, and our future plans for a summer vacation. We both knew that my pheasant-hunting trip wasn't the right thing. I just wasn't man enough to do the right thing on my own, so I asked Jamie for permission. In doing so, I put her in a no-win situation; if she said yes, she'd be going against what was right and what was according to her conscience. If she said no, then she would be made the bad guy. The fun killer. The party stopper.

Our wives weren't intended to be our mothers. Men need to listen to their inner compass, their conscience, and decide for themselves what is right and what is wrong. When we want something that, if we're honest with ourselves, we know isn't the best choice and we make our wives tell us no, we're making them play a parent role in the relationship. Simply put, a child-parent relationship isn't the same thing as a husband-wife relationship.

Sometimes, for men, the best decision is not to run to the wilderness. And we need to make that decision ourselves, without placing our wives in the mother role.

Sometimes it's good to ask for permission. Sometimes it's the wrong thing to do. A wise man will make the call based on what will honor his wife.

God gave us the wild, rugged, isolated places for several great purposes. They declare His power and His glory. They provide the beauty, challenge, or undistracted loneliness that help us to listen well. Nothing can replace the wilderness as a means of being refreshed, inspired, and renewed. Zealous men should run to wild, rugged, isolated places as often as God, their families, and their consciences allow. Sometimes alone. Sometimes with our wives, families, and friends.

Always with the untamable God who made our untamed lands.

**Really great people make you feel that
you, too, can become great.**

—MARK TWAIN

13

MAKING OTHERS GREAT

I t's counterintuitive. It conflicts with almost every commercial, billboard, and marketing jingle. It's not the popular path. Yet truly masculine men live well *by living for others*.

Bono's dedication to fighting poverty and hunger in Third World countries. Tony Dungy's commitment to helping fathers connect with their sons. Gary Haugen's passionate commitment to securing justice for victims of slavery and sexual exploitation around the world. These are just a few examples of men who live to serve others.

If it weren't for the real-life example set for me by my father-in-law, RB Drickey, I'm not sure I would have understood this truth. RB is one of the hardest-working, most ambitious men I've ever known. Yet his best energy typically goes toward empowering others to live well.

When RB was eighteen, his father died of cancer. RB was in his first semester of college, making new friends and good grades. Wayne State College was an exciting change from the small farm town he'd grown up in.

The Friday after Thanksgiving break, RB's dad, the town's grocer, was diagnosed with lung cancer. When RB returned a month later for Christmas break, his father was too sick to run the store. RB stayed home from his second semester in college to help run the store while his dad received treatments. He planned to manage Drickey's Market for six months and then return to school the next fall.

Plans changed. RB buried his father in a frozen cemetery on a cold day that next February, just three months after his dad's initial diagnosis. The year was 1967, and RB has managed Drickey's Market ever since.

The decision to stay home from school and wear the grocer's hat was a complicated one. RB was zealous, intelligent, and hardworking. When he'd left for college, he felt that the world had opened up before him. But even at eighteen years of age, he had a fatherly, protective heart. When he considered his mother, his sister, and the employees at the store, he felt a strong sense of responsibility. RB has cut meat, stocked shelves, and managed a grocery store for nearly four decades with no feelings of regret or self-pity.

RB's story resembles George Bailey's from the movie *It's a Wonderful Life*. In that film, George, a small-town boy fresh out of high school, longs to see the world. While talking to Mary, his girlfriend, he says, "I'm shaking the dust of this crummy little town off my feet and I'm gonna see the world. Italy, Greece, the Parthenon, the Colosseum. Then I'm coming back here to go to college and see what they know. And then I'm gonna build things. I'm gonna build air fields, I'm gonna build skyscrapers a hundred stories high, I'm gonna build bridges a mile long."

Then George's father has a fatal stroke. After counting the cost, George decides to stay home and run the Bailey Building and Loan Association so that his brother, Harry, can go to college. George even gives Harry his own college savings to help pay for Harry's education. Throughout the movie, George continually sets aside his personal aspirations and goals in order to chase other people's dreams.

George doesn't understand how valuable he's been to those around him until he is given a glimpse of what Bedford Falls would have looked like had he not existed. In that alternative reality *without George*, the town is dull and lifeless. Greedy people are in charge. The town is in poor shape. George gains a sense of how his decisions to put others first benefited people in life-giving ways. Everyone in Bedford Falls is better off for having known this zealous, ambitious, other-centered man.

In my opinion, the same thing can be said about RB Drickey. Like George Bailey, if there is something RB can do to help others, he'll do it. In the 1970s, a man from town declared bankruptcy. Shortly after filing the papers, Fred applied to work at Drickey's Market. A couple of months into his employment, Fred had a stroke and had to take four months off from work to recover. His insurance company refused to pay his medical or living expenses, which, with a wife and four young children, put Fred in an impossible situation.

RB talked it over with his wife, and they decided to pay this man's wages while he recovered. One day, when RB was making a deposit, the banker pulled him aside and said, "You're acting crazy, Drickey. You'll go broke. You know that, don't ya?"

RB could live with the idea of going broke. What he couldn't live with was the idea of someone else struggling if there was something he could do to help.

Few people have been more generous or helpful to me than my father-in-law. For example, when Jamie and I were in our first year of marriage, we decided that I would go to seminary. Two weeks after making that decision, an investment statement showed up in the mail. A mutual fund in Jamie's name held $24,000.

When I saw the statement, I asked Jamie about it. She told me that the money belonged to her parents. She explained how, from the time she was born, RB and her mom, Bev, had invested $75 a month into a "future dreams" account for her. Jamie had paid for college from that fund, but since she was now out of school and married, she had assumed that the money would return to her parents.

She assumed incorrectly. When she called her dad, he said, "No, Jamie, that's *your* money. Your mother and I set a little bit aside every month, from the time you were born, so that you could use it to follow your dreams. Now that you're married, you and Zeke can use it however you see best."

We paid for three years of seminary with those funds. But they did more than cover tuition. Because we didn't need to pay for school, Jamie was able to accept a lesser-paying job on campus, working with people who shared her passion for philosophy and Christian apologetics. Because she worked on campus, we made the same friends, had lunch together, and went through those three years together. Those were three of the most formative, enjoyable years of our lives, largely made possible because RB and his wife, Bev, made a commitment twenty-four years earlier to help Jamie chase her dreams.

THE BEST EXEMPLAR

It's inspiring to be served in such generous ways. Examples like RB give men a picture of what it looks like to put others first. Yet I realize that many men don't have an RB in their lives. I recently met with a young husband and father, Shawn, whose dad and father-in-law have been "absent dads." Now that these fathers are grandfathers, they are absent grandfathers. They don't send birthday presents to their grandchildren. They don't visit often. They rarely ask Shawn about his family.

Shawn and I have searched and searched, but we haven't been able to find a single exemplar in his family. Naturally, Shawn struggled with the vision to be other-centered. He had a hundred questions about what it looked like to put others first but not many answers.

There is one example that is available to everyone. RB has done a fantastic job of helping me understand what it looks like to put others first, but he's not my primary example. He's not the one that I *most* pattern my life after. For me, Jesus is the one who takes all of the vague, abstract ideas of how to love others and puts flesh, blood, bone, and sinews to them. Jesus concretizes the idea of chasing others' dreams.

Shawn's been reading the Gospels, and it's been filling out his picture. Matthew, Mark, Luke, and John have provided us with dozens of accounts of Jesus chasing other people's dreams. Real people. Hurting people. People discarded and ignored by the world. Like when Jesus healed the man with a withered hand (Luke 6:6–11). Or when He healed the servant of a Roman military officer (Luke 7:1–10). Then there's the moment when He felt Mary and Martha's sadness over the death of their brother, and He cried with them. Then, after crying, He filled Lazarus's lungs once again with the breath of life.

One of my favorite examples of Jesus chasing another person's dreams is the story of the Samaritan woman at the well (John 4). This woman was thirsty but not for what the well offered. She'd lived a hard, tragic life. She'd been marginalized by society in every way a person could be marginalized. She was a woman, at a time in which women were viewed as dirty, lesser creatures. She was a Samaritan, a member of a nation viewed by the Jews as defiled. And according to Jewish law, she was a sinner. She'd been married five different times. At the time when she encountered Jesus, a different man, perhaps soon to be number six, waited for this woman to return with her pot of water.

This woman would have been viewed as a cultural by-product, an outcast. No self-respecting Jewish rabbi on his way to Jerusalem would have stopped to talk with her.

But Jesus did. He stopped, sat down, and shared the kingdom of God with her. The woman was so energized by this man that she raced home and told everyone in her village about Jesus. They listened to her. Then they listened to Jesus, "and many more believed because of his word" (John 4:41).

It would be easy to miss the depth of what Jesus accomplished for this woman by having that simple conversation with her. But in that moment, Jesus changed everything for her. He gave her dignity and a sense of value, showing her that

God has a heart for women, just as He does for men. Jesus also elevated her worth in the eyes of her community. Jesus restored her to her village when He chose her to be the catalyst for a spiritual revolution. I imagine that the next twenty, thirty, perhaps forty years of that woman's life were transformed because of Jesus.

The pages of the New Testament are filled with stories about this man who had a simple agenda: to love God with all His being and love His neighbor as Himself (Matthew 22:37–40).

If men lack vision and motivation, they need only to pick up their Bibles and read. Jesus will fill them with all of the vivid pictures and energizing motivations that they need to do some chasing.

TWO DEFINITIONS OF GREATNESS

Many have said that you can judge the stature of a man by what he's accomplished *for himself*. Yet the tallest trees in the kingdom of God are men who spend their lives accomplishing things *for others*.

There's an untraversable chasm between the world's definition of greatness and God's. Ambitious men have struggled with this distinction for thousands of years. Two of Jesus's friends, James and John, the fishermen brothers from Capernaum, got it backward. They wanted to be men of honor. They wanted to be respected. They wanted to sit in positions of high esteem. Sounds familiar, right?

In some ways, James and John *were* already great men. While most people walked away from Jesus baffled and confused, these two brothers had grasped the idea that He was Israel's promised Messiah. That's admirable faith. What's more, it was that faith that led them to make their request of Jesus. Because they believed that Jesus would be crowned Israel's king soon and would, like all kings, get to choose whom to honor, they requested: "Grant us to sit, one at your right hand and one at your left, in your glory" (Mark 10:37).

Preachers have criticized James and John for two thousand years for making that request. Dozens of sermons have made these fishermen sound like selfish monsters for desiring greatness. They are not selfish monsters; they are human. The desire for greatness is in the heart of man because God put it there.

What's more, their request was perfectly natural according to the world's definition of greatness. In the world's economy, James and John deserved what they'd asked for.

Think about what these men left behind to follow Jesus. While scores of people were turning away from Jesus, or plotting ways to kill Him, these two men left their father, the family trade, their friends, and their hometown. They linked their entire reputation to the life of this eccentric man from Nazareth. Again, that's admirable faith and loyalty. Now that Jesus was at the threshold of His glory, these devoted followers naturally expected to receive greater glory, too.

This is how it works in the world.

Long before George W. Bush became the forty-third president of the United States, he was part owner of the Texas Rangers baseball team. A young man, Israel Hernandez, was fresh out of college from a small Texas town named Eagle Pass. Bush and Hernandez became friends, and Hernandez admired

Bush so much that he drove around the state of Texas helping to promote the Rangers organization.

Several years later, when Bush "came into his kingdom" as president, he remembered his friends. Those who'd been loyal were shown loyalty. Dozens of Bush's "Jameses and Johns" were given exalted positions, titles, and salaries. Bush appointed Hernandez to the role of assistant secretary of commerce, giving him the privilege of traveling around the world promoting free trade.[1] Each president, Democrat or Republican, has similar stories of rewarding loyalty.

Loyalty, faith, and commitment are often rewarded in this world with greatness of money, respect, and authority. So, before we preach one more "look at these greedy fools" sermon against James and John, we should appreciate how appropriate their request was, according to the world's definition of greatness. There's a good chance that I would have asked for the same honor.

Which means that I would have needed the same corrective. While Jesus didn't rebuke James's and John's desire for greatness, He did redefine their definition. Jesus replied, "You know that those who are considered rulers of the Gentiles lord it over them, and their great ones exercise authority over them" (Mark 10:42). Greatness in the world is a hierarchy. Great men rule lesser men. According to the world of men, the higher up the ladder you climb, the more people you get to boss around.

This isn't how it works in God's kingdom. Jesus said, "But it shall not be so among you. But whoever would be great among you must be your servant, and whoever would be first among you must be slave of all" (Mark 10:43–44).

This is radical stuff. Jesus doesn't just modify the definition of greatness with that statement. He didn't merely adjust the path toward honor and glory. He flipped the world's entire system of greatness on its ear. He especially toppled the system with what He said next. Jesus says about Himself, "For even the Son of Man came not to be served but to serve, and to give his life as a ransom for many" (Mark 10:45).

Consider the implications of that last statement. If Jesus, the most infinitely worthy, authoritative, and "great" man this world has ever known, *came to serve*, what does greatness look like for us?

THE ZERO-REGRET PURSUIT

Some may feel that chasing others' dreams is an overwhelming idea. Some will likely assume that their plate is too full as it is without adding one more pursuit.

Chasing others' dreams is actually the one passionate pursuit that can add clarity and simplicity to your entire life. As I write this chapter, my wife and I are preparing to sell our house. We're also working on an addition to our new house, which we just purchased in the country. I'm coaching my son's baseball team, training my dog, and exercising four times a week. I'm like many zealous men; I'm trying to live out successfully dozens of priorities and relationships. Several times a week, I feel fragmented and exhausted.

For earnest, hardworking men, this multiplicity of priorities and relationships can feel overwhelming. Every day presents dozens of choices about how to invest our time and energy. *Good* choices. There's no question that playing catch with our children, working, exercising, taking our wives on dates, changing the oil in our vehicles, or mowing our lawns are all excellent options. In fact, that's what makes life feel so complicated. When we survey our options, we can't simply ask the question *What's worth my time and energy?* We have to grapple with the harder, more difficult question, *What's* most *worth my time and energy?*

That question can give men insomnia. I had a bad night a couple of years ago. I'd felt tired from the moment I got home from work that afternoon. I'd yawned through dinner, through playing games with the kids, and then through reading by the fireplace. At ten o'clock, I dragged myself up the stairs and into bed. The second I got horizontal, my mind started spinning like a pinwheel. I started thinking about all of the ways I was failing as a husband, father, pastor, and friend. All I could think about were the people in my life who mattered the most and how disappointed they must be with me.

I know that I'm not alone. Many men feel anxiety about important responsibilities or relationships. I shared the story of my restless night while speaking at a men's event last year. After the event, a line of men formed behind the stage. One man after another told me that he felt the same way.

I'll never forget the last guy in line, a man in his fifties. He was a short, plump man with a white beard and a look of worry on his face. He told me, "My biggest fear is that I'll reach the end of my life and realize that I blew it. I wish that there was a way to simplify it all down . . . so that I could know at all times that I'm living well."

He wanted a simple, clarifying focus for his life. That might sound like a tall order, but it isn't. When men run hard and energetically after what's best for the people in their lives, they'll never go wrong. Helping others chase their dreams is a zero-regret pursuit.

As a pastor, I've had the privilege of hearing the thoughts and feelings of several men in their last days. Two strong themes have emerged from listening to dying people. First, everyone feels some regret about things he did or didn't do with his life. Some people have strong regrets. Some have relatively small ones. But everyone has some type of answer to the question "What would you do *differently*, if you had the chance?"

Just yesterday, I met with a husband whose wife was in her last days. Ray left the care facility where his wife, Lorraine, was on life support to meet me in my office and discuss her funeral plans. Ray was old and would likely follow his bride into eternity shortly after she left. As we met, he mentioned a few things that he wished he could go back and do differently. I told him that those feelings are common. We all face some regrets; that's one theme.

The second theme is that nobody regrets the time he spent putting others first. I talked with Ray for about an hour. He told me the story of his life and marriage to Lorraine. But not once did he say something like "I wish I wouldn't have taken my wife on that special anniversary trip" or "If could go back in time, I wouldn't have spent so much energy getting to know my wife and her dreams and then making them happen." I didn't hear those thoughts from Ray, and I've never heard them from any husband, because nobody second-guesses the time he's spent helping other people.

Making others great is *the* zero-regret pursuit that simplifies and clarifies all other pursuits. If men love well, everything they do is in focus and counts, regardless of the outcome. If men don't love well, then even their moments of greatest accomplishment are meaningless. For zealous, hyper-hobbied, pursuit-driven men, the ambition to chase others' dreams is vital. It simplifies all relationships and priorities. It shows us what choice we should make, in the middle of the gauntlet, in order to live without regrets.

The choice to love well is the choice to live well.

In dreams begin responsibility.

—WILLIAM BUTLER YEATS

**Don't forget what happened to the
man who suddenly got everything he always
wanted. . . . He lived happily ever after.**

—WILLY WONKA

14

DRIVEN BY DREAMS

MOTIVATING IMAGES

O f the two of us, my dad is the runner. His long legs and efficient strides carry him with grace over the jogging paths of Lincoln, Nebraska. I look like a knuckle-dragging yeti when we run together. I start complaining, panting, and shuffling my feet before we leave the driveway.

It was 10:30 in the morning and ninety degrees outside. My legs felt like overboiled pasta. I was logging fifteen miles in order to meet a goal, which, at three miles out, I hated myself for setting.

Six months earlier, I'd sent in a deposit for an archery grizzly hunt in Alaska. That same week, in an ambitious moment, I'd said to my dad, "Hey, how about running the Grand Island half-marathon together in August?" Running a half seemed like a good way to prepare for the challenge of hiking mountains in the tundra state. Later that day, I registered online, reserving an extra-large T-shirt and a place at the starting gate. The

15-miler was the "long run" my dad suggested we get in before race day.

I glanced at my dad, hoping to see exhaustion on his face, but it wasn't there. As I said, he's the runner. Not only was he not grimacing, but his lips were curved into a grin of satisfaction. *How irritating,* I thought. *I'm dying one, slow, miserable step at a time, and my dad's prancing along as if it were mile number one.* He was obviously enjoying one of his proudest moments as a father—the initiation of his son into the fraternity of distance runners.

Or so he thought.

"I'm done, Dad. I give up." By the time I said "up," I'd collapsed in the shade of one of the Austrian pines lining the jogging path. My dad slowed, circled back, and returned to crouch by my head.

"Come on, bud. Only three miles. The barn door's open." He always used this phrase on our shorter runs when we made the last turn and could see our house. Sometimes it sparked off a sprint to the finish. This time, it was only irritating.

"You're not hearing me, Dad. I can't." I felt surprisingly peaceful, almost euphoric, lying on the soft grass and looking up through the pine branches.

"All right, you lie there a couple of minutes while I tell you about the finish," he said.

I grunted, warning him that his attempt to nudge me would likely fail.

"Here's what'll happen," he said. "We'll rest a couple of minutes, then you'll get up and we'll knock out these last piddly miles. When we get home, we'll head straight for the pool. We'll kick off our shoes and jump in, clothes and all. Your mom will bring us a couple of sports drinks on ice, and we'll bob around in the cold water."

"Go on," I said in a *slightly* less defensive tone.

"When we're cooled off, I'll fix you a huge plate of smoked pork with Gates Bar-B-Q sauce. We'll eat until we're stuffed, with no guilt, because we just ran fifteen miles!"

He let the picture sink in a moment and then asked, "So, what do you think? You up for finishing?"

Two and a half minutes earlier, I knew I was done running for the day. In fact, I was never moving from that soft, relaxing spot on the grass—ever! I was going to raise my kids, build my house, and retire on that plot of turf. But the dream did its work, and now I was standing to my feet to put them through thirty more minutes of pavement pounding in the sweltering heat. All because of the picture of the finish my dad painted for me.

Active, hard-charging men are driven by dreams. When they can picture how an activity will bring them closer to the future they desire, they have sufficient motivation to carry it out. If they lack dreams, they lack energy.

Dreams can be as short-term as jumping into a swimming pool after a long, hot workout. They can also be as distant as the way we'd like to finish life, with our family by our side, feeling a sense of accomplishment and satisfaction. Dreams are pictures of the future, images of what we hope to actualize and experience.

I was moved to action several times today by dreams of the future. After work, I stopped by the grocery store to pick up a bundle of cilantro so that I could make salsa. Imagining the moment when my family would stand around the counter, dipping chip after chip into a bowl of fresh tomatoes, peppers, onions, cilantro, and lime juice, carried me to my local grocery. However, before I went to the store, I stopped by my investment agent's office and opened up a new retirement account. The idea of having money set aside to help put our children through college or take trips to Ireland, India, and Italy with Jamie in thirty years motivated me to do something rather dull.

Future dreams—salsa tonight and Ireland when I'm seventy— compelled me to action. Yet a lack of vision caused me to neglect several other activities. I didn't exercise today. I didn't mow my lawn. I didn't even hang up my khakis when I got home from work; I tossed them over the shower-curtain rod, threw on a pair of shorts, and raced into the kitchen to chop veggies. I probably should have mowed my lawn, jogged three miles, and hung up my pants, but because some dreams were more energizing than others, my family got a bowl of garden-fresh salsa but had to put up with a messy bathroom and a lawn that looked like Nebraska's native prairie.

GRABBING THE BEST DREAMS

Zealous men know how to dream. They prove this point with the unending energy they have for certain pursuits. Men will spend long hours in the garage, as they picture heads turning when they drive through town in the purring, shimmering car they rebuilt. Imagining financial success and the respect of an employer motivates some men to be consistently the last to leave the office. The image of showing my kids a massive set of elk antlers motivates me to work hard—studying mountain ranges, organizing my gear, and practicing with my bow each week.

Dreaming is easy. The challenge lies in choosing the best dreams. In *Ordering Your Private World*, Gordon MacDonald recounts a conversation he had with his father: "Years ago my father suggested that one of the great tests of human character is found in making critical choices of selection and rejection amidst all of the opportunities that lurk in life's path. 'Your challenge,' he told me, 'will not be in separating out the good from the bad, but in grabbing the best out of all the possible good.'"[1]

If there's one thing that God loves to do, it's help men trade smallish, empty dreams for big, challenging, life-demanding ones. A life of small dreams is a wasted life. There is no thrill in climbing low mountains.

No man has to live a wasted life. If a man turns his life over to God through faith, there is no limit to the turnaround that is possible. When a man chooses to live by grace through faith, bigger dreams will be found, and lives will be changed.

I've watched God empower several men to trade in small dreams for bigger ones, low mountains for grand ones. Perhaps no story is more dramatic than my friend Brad's. Five years ago, Brad grabbed hold of a better vision for his life.

At that time, Brad had been married to Marcia for ten years. They had five sons younger than nine. For the first eight years of their marriage, Brad had been away from home three months out of the year for work or play. Among the ranks of over-the-top, fanatical men, Brad was close to number one. As a young man, he was a Marine[2] whose worst fear had been inactivity, so he'd filled his time with fast, dangerous, and expensive ways to stave it off. Over the course of his lifetime, he'd owned seven Harley-Davidson motorcycles, scuba-dived boat wrecks in the Bahamas, Greece, and Mexico, and competitively raced demolition-derby cars. He'd been a gym rat, a bodybuilder on steroids who lived in the weight room. At his peak, Brad stood five-foot-seven and weighed 248 pounds. He had 6 percent body fat and bench-pressed 450 pounds.

Brad had a picture of where his happiness in life would come from, but his dream was trashing his liver and his relationships. A few family members tried to help. Most people simply stayed out of his way. Brad said, "If people interfered with what I wanted, I'd run over them."

That was Brad a few years ago. Today, he's participating faithfully in our community. I use him as an example of a committed husband and father when I counsel other men. Marcia is one of the most happily married women in our church. She just asked me on Sunday, "Zeke, would you invite Brad to go fishing with you the next time you go? He's so focused on being good to me and the kids I'm worried that he's not having enough fun." After the smelling salts returned me to consciousness, I told Marcia that I've never heard a wife complain that her husband wasn't goofing off enough.

I treated Brad to a cup of coffee to discuss his changes. Brad explained how it began with a painful epiphany on his son's fourth birthday: "Jordan woke up excited for his birthday party. He raced into the kitchen before breakfast and said, 'Mom, today's going to be so great, isn't it? Everyone will be at my party, right? Everyone *but Dad,* of course.'"

"Everyone but Dad, of course." That comment took Brad into the shadows. He realized that he hadn't been a good dad. He'd been absent from everything. He had almost no memories of connecting with Jordan. As unbelievable as it sounds, Brad couldn't remember a single birthday, soccer game, or time that he'd snuggled, wrestled, or played catch with his son. He told me, "My son had been alive for four years, and I didn't know him."

Brad felt miserable all day. He told me, "I'll never forget what happened later that night. After Jordan fell asleep, tired out from his big day, I snuck into his bedroom. I sat down on the edge of his bed, and watched him sleep for a few moments. I rubbed his head and began to cry. I whispered over and over again how sorry I was. He was asleep, but it didn't matter. I had to keep apologizing."

That's how it all began, but it didn't end there. When Jordan's comment sobered him, Brad realized that there were dozens of other relationships and responsibilities that he'd neglected. For some reason, he started to care. He started to feel pain and regret. Marines don't like to cry, but this one dropped quite a few tears over the next several days as he faced his mistakes.

Ken Gire writes, "So much is distilled in our tears, not the least of which is wisdom in living life. From my own tears I have learned that if you follow your tears, you will find your heart. If you find your heart, you will find what is dear to God. And if you find what is dear to God, you will find the answer to how you should live your life."[3]

Brad's pain and regret forced him into a period of serious scrutiny. He began to pray and ask God for help. He also began to read the Scriptures for direction. He told me, "I needed a vision, Zeke. So I began to read the Gospels and Paul's letters to get a picture of how I should live."

One of the passages from the Bible that gave Brad a new dream was Matthew 22:37–40, where Jesus tells a group of religious leaders that the entire law of God can be summarized in two commandments: "You shall love the Lord your God with all your heart and with all your soul and with all your mind. This is the great and first commandment. And a second is like it: You shall love your neighbor as yourself. On these two commandments depend all the Law and the Prophets."

Brad said, "I read those words, and I realized that they perfectly described how I wanted to live the rest of my life. I needed to live for my God and the people in my life. No more selfishness. No more running over others. That passage gave me a bigger picture to chase."

That painful period in Brad's life led to new commitments and plans. When he began to feel crushed under the weight of his failures, he turned to Jesus. He asked for forgiveness for years of selfishness and the hurt he'd caused. Because of Jesus's life and death, Brad found forgiveness. Brad found the Grace Story. Like the example of my son, Aidan, playing outside as a clean, forgiven, deeply loved child, grace sent Brad back into his life with fresh energy and a new set of hopes and expectations.

Brad is an even harder-charging, more ambitious man today than he was five years ago. He just has a powerful, life-giving pursuit that he's chasing now: loving God and loving others well.

At the end of our talk, Brad told me, "I used to wake up and think, 'I can't wait until I can go coon hunting tonight or duck hunting this weekend.' Now I wake up, consider my options, and tell myself, 'I can't wait to be the kind of father today who helps my boys grow up to love God and do what is right. I can't wait to be the kind of husband who makes Marcia feel loved and like we're on the same team."

I asked Brad if life is better today. He replied, "Are you kidding? I'm *finally* living the dream!"

FLESH-SCRAPING PAIN

While it's true that Brad's life changed in dramatic ways, he's not unique. I've watched God reorient dozens of men in similar ways. It's what He does. He takes broken-out-of-the-box men, flips them around, and expands their dreams. This is exciting stuff, worth the pain.

But it almost always takes pain. When God reforms and re-shapes a man's life, it's typically not a fun experience for the man. Much like having a boil scraped off or a tooth extracted, the transformation of our hearts is not fun.

In C. S. Lewis's book *The Voyage of the Dawn Treader*, Eustace experienced such a transformation. At the book's opening, he was a whiny, self-centered, obnoxious young man. Partway into the book, Eustace was transformed into a dragon. This change humbled him and helped him see how ugly he had been. It cre-ated a longing inside for a second chance at life.

Living as a dragon forced Eustace to assess his life and decide who he wanted to be. He reformed his dreams. Then, once these internal changes took place, he was changed back into a human, a better version of his old self, with the help of Aslan the lion.

But the change from a dragon back to his reoriented human form was an excruciatingly painful experience. Here's how Lewis describes the moment:

> Then the lion said—but I don't know if it spoke—"You will have to let me undress you." I was afraid of his claws, I can tell you, but I was pretty near desperate now. So I just lay flat down on my back to let him do it.
>
> The very first tear he made was so deep that I

thought it had gone right into my heart. And when he began pulling the skin off, it hurt worse than anything I've ever felt. The only thing that made me able to bear it was just the pleasure of feeling the stuff peel off. You know—if you've ever picked the scab off a sore place. It hurts like billy—oh but it is such fun to see it coming away.[4]

To trade smaller dreams for larger, life-giving ones, men need to think deeply about their lives, their relationships, and their commitments. As Eustace was forced to do, men need to live inside their dragons, soberly recognizing the pain they've caused themselves and others. Then, in that sobriety and humility, they need to meet with God in their brokenness. Men are never alone in the shadowlands. God is always there, ready and waiting to walk men through their pain and regret.

Trading in smaller dreams for larger ones is not fun stuff, nor is it easy. But it's the process that leads to changed lives, lives characterized by love, significance, and deep, healthy relationships. Ask Brad, and he'd tell you that finding his new life was worth all of the pain the process required.

DREAMS THAT WORK

What dreams are you living? Are they the *best* ones? Or are they lesser dreams that need to be traded up for better ones? To answer those questions, men need only to examine whether their dreams supply energy for their most important values and relationships. Viktor Frankl said, "The common trait of all emotionally healthy people is a desire to get to work." The best dreams create a desire in men to get to work on the things that matter most.

Are your dreams motivating you to grow closer to the God who loves you? Are they inspiring you to work on your marriage, your parenting, or your involvement in your local church or community? Or are they removing your motivation to work on the important things in life?

Zealous men sometimes need help asking and answering these questions. Men caught up in a passionate pursuit are good at rationalizing. This is where community—our family and friends—is invaluable. My wife, Jamie, and my closest friends know my dreams. My *best* dreams. They know that I want to have nothing in my life that is more important to me than Jesus. They know that I want a marriage that reflects the relationship that Jesus has with the church. They know that I want to be the kind of dad who coaches my son's T-ball team, reads stories to my kids before bed, and attends every ballet and piano recital. I never want anyone to describe Zeke Pipher as "absent."

My wife and friends also know that I'm easily thrown off balance. Men who live by grace still slip up, and they're sometimes the last to see it or, at least, to admit it. A couple of years ago, I overcommitted myself to writing projects. In addition to my work as a pastor, I'm a freelance outdoor writer and photographer. In the fall of 2007, several deadlines came due at the same time. I'd lock up the church, drive home, and work at my laptop until bedtime. If the kids came up to me to show me a picture they colored or a rock they found in our yard, I'd shoo them away, saying, "Daddy's writing. Please don't interrupt me."

I've been married to Jamie for thirteen years, and she's never scolded me. She doesn't complain or coerce. She asks questions. Jamie heard me ask the kids to stop bothering me, and as soon as they were out of the room, she said, "I love it that you're finding so much success with your outdoor writing. I'm proud of you. But do you think these articles are keeping you from the success you want to have as a father?"

Ouch. A sour taste formed in the back of my throat. The answer slammed into my conscience the instant she asked the question. I'd let a lesser dream outcompete a greater one.

I wasn't bitter at Jamie for asking this question. I was embarrassed for not catching this conflict of priorities on my own. But this is how passionate men operate. We tend to throw it into high gear and race forward as fast as the machine will allow. When an exciting, consuming pursuit comes along, we slip on the blinders and run after it with undeterred attention.

Hard-charging men need families and friends who know them well and are committed to their long-term success. But we need to give them permission to ask questions and offer advice. Members of my close community understand my dreams; we've had countless talks about them. They're also familiar with my ability to subvert my dreams and work against myself. I know my friends' dreams and missteps, too. We're committed to one another. We've given ourselves permission to lean in and challenge one another on how well we're accomplishing our priorities. We'll meet at the archery range or for a cup of coffee, and we'll ask one another questions about our marriages, parenting, and work. We'll ask direct questions about our thoughts, choices, and behaviors. There are many areas in which men can fail morally; we've given ourselves permission to probe these areas and surface the truth.

Even with this permission, it still takes courage to challenge a man. Like a hungry dog that's been deprived of a meaty bone, men tend to get a bit growly when they are kept from a passionate pursuit. Accountability relationships aren't easy or safe, but they're essential to helping zealous men stay on track. A man who finishes life well is a man who ran his race with committed, courageous friends.

IN DREAMS BEGIN RESPONSIBILITY

A few months ago, our family got a German wirehair puppy. In the morning, when Ezra hears my footsteps crossing the kitchen floor toward his kennel, he wags his tail so hard against the plastic it sounds like a drum roll. When I open the front door, he bounds outside with the energy of fifty dogs. He never tires. We could play fetch for an hour, and he'd never slow down. His feet, soaked with the morning dew, barely touch the ground as he flies after the rubber bumper over and over again. Our training sessions are pure pleasure for him.

This is what men want. They want to race with boundless, inexhaustible energy after *all* of their priorities. Not just bass fishing and geo-caching. Not just work or exercise. Not just golf or rebuilding old cars. Men want to experience energy and enthusiasm toward each of their important relationships and responsibilities. Men want to feel successful in every way. They want to "live the dream," as my friend Brad put it.

This can happen for you. If you choose to dream well. As William Butler Yeats said, "In dreams begin responsibility."

ENDNOTES

CHAPTER ONE

[1]Associated Press (May 29, 2006). "Fight club draws techies for bloody underground beatdowns," *USA Today.* Retrieved on April 28, 2007.

[2]Bruce Rosenstein, (August 1, 2006). "Illegal, violent teen fight clubs face police crackdown," *USA Today.* Retrieved on April 28, 2007.

[3]John Eldredge, *Wild at Heart: Discovering the Secret of a Man's Soul* (Nashville: Thomas Nelson, 2001), p. 5.

[4]Neal Bascomb, *The Perfect Mile* (Boston: Houghton Mifflin, 2004), pp. 10–11 of prologue.

[5]David M. Ewalt with Lacey Rose, "Bannister's Four-Minute Mile Named Greatest Athletic Achievement," http://www.forbes.com/2005/11/18/bannister-four-minute-mile_cx_de_lr_1118bannister.html.

[6]"Addict." Merriam-Webster Online Dictionary. Merriam-Webster Online, http://www.merriam-webster.com/dictionary/addict.

CHAPTER THREE

[1]"Death from Laughter" on Wikipedia, the Free Encyclopedia. Website: http://en.wikipedia.org/wiki/Fatal_hilarity.

CHAPTER FOUR

[1]Peter Kreeft, *Christianity for Modern Pagans: Pascal's Pensées Edited, Outlined, and Explained* (San Francisco: Ignatius Press, 1993), p. 168.

CHAPTER FIVE

[1]Frederick Buechner, *Wishful Thinking: A Seeker's ABC*, revised and expanded (San Francisco: Harper, 1993), p. 65.

CHAPTER SIX

[1]Wendell Berry, "Feminism, the Body, and the Machine" in *What Are People For? Essays by Wendell Berry* (New York: North Point Press, 1990), p. 184.

[2]Dallas Willard, *Renovation of the Heart: Putting on the Character of Christ* (Colorado Springs, CO: NavPress, 2002), p. 142.

[3]Ibid., p. 142.

[4]Eric Marrapodi, " 'Christian Famous' Pastor Quits His Church, Moves to Asia" on CNN.com's Belief Blog. Web address: http://religion.blogs.cnn.com/2010/12/22/"christian-famous"-pastor-quits-his-church-moves-to-asia/

CHAPTER SEVEN

[1]Mike Mason, *The Mystery of Marriage: Meditations on the Miracle* (Sisters, OR: Multnomah, 1985), p. 109.

[2]http://www.barna.org/barna-update/article/15-familykids/42-new-marriage-and-divorce-statistics-released.

CHAPTER EIGHT

[1]Mary Pipher, *Seeking Peace: Chronicles of the Worst Buddhist in the World* (New York: Riverhead Books, 2009), p. 67.

[2]Nathan Miller, *Theodore Roosevelt: A Life* (New York: HarperCollins, 2003), p. 32.

[3]Ibid.

CHAPTER NINE

[1]David Wexler, "Shame-O-Phobia," in *Psychotherapy Networker*, May/June 2010, p. 23.

[2]Scott Swain, "Covert Intimacy: Closeness in Men's Friendships," in *Gender in Intimate Relationships*, ed. Barbara Risman and Pepper Schwartz (Belmont, CA: Wadsworth, 1989), pp. 71–86.

[3]Henri Nouwen, *Intimacy* (New York: HarperCollins, 1969).

CHAPTER TEN

[1]Eugene Peterson, *Christ Plays in Ten Thousand Places: A Conversation in Spiritual Theology* (Grand Rapids, MI: Eerdmans, 2005), p. 250.
[2]Ibid., p. 226.

CHAPTER ELEVEN

[1]Dallas Willard, *Renovation of the Heart: Putting on the Character of Christ* (Colorado Springs, CO: NavPress, 2002), p. 179.
[2]Stephen Mansfield, *The Search for God and Guinness: A Biography of the Beer that Changed the World* (Nashville: Thomas Nelson, 2009), p. 111.
[3]Ibid., p. 118.

CHAPTER TWELVE

[1]"ερημος, ον," in Walter Bauer, *A Greek-English Lexicon of the New Testament and Other Early Christian Literature*, second edition (Chicago: University of Chicago Press, 1979), p. 309.
[2]John Eldredge, *Wild at Heart: Discovering the Secret of a Man's Soul* (Nashville: Thomas Nelson, 2001), p. 19.
[3]Mike Mason, *The Mystery of Marriage: Meditations on the Miracle* (Sisters, OR: Multnomah, 1985), p. 167.

CHAPTER THIRTEEN

[1]Sheryl Gay Stolberg, "Bush Friends, Loyal and Texan, Remain a Force," published February 21, 2007. Taken from the website: http://www.nytimes.com/2007/02/21/washington/21loyalists.html.

CHAPTER FOURTEEN

[1]Gordon MacDonald, *Ordering Your Private World* (Nashville: Thomas Nelson, 2003), p. 96.
[2]When Brad read and approved his story, his one stipulation was that I affirm the idea that "once a Marine, always a Marine." I used the past tense only for grammatical purposes.
[3]Ken Gire, *Windows of the Soul* (Grand Rapids, MI: Zondervan, 1996), p. 195.
[4]C. S. Lewis, *The Voyage of the Dawn Treader* (New York: HarperCollins, 1952), pp. 115–16.

AUTHOR QUESTIONNAIRE

A CONVERSATION WITH DR. ZEKE PIPHER

1. You discuss the moment you realized that after nine years of marriage your wife still wasn't entirely sure of your commitment to your family. Was this moment also your impetus for deciding to write *Man on the Run*? Is the theme of impassioned men and their difficulty in committing to their families something you'd already been interested in from your sessions with parishioners?

It's hard to put a finger on when and why light switches finally turn on inside our hearts. Watching the old sportsman (described in the introduction to *Man on the Run*) die with such strong feelings of shame and regret made a deep impression on me. It seems that when God wants to teach me something, He creates themes in my life. At the same time this sportsman was dying in shame, I started hearing more comments from my wife and children about my absence. I was also helping several men in counseling who were dealing with severe pain caused by their pursuits. All these things together seemed to flip a switch. I sat down to write *Man on the Run* primarily because I wanted to think deeply about these things for myself.

2. **Through your work as a pastor, you have been witness to the inner lives of many people in your counseling sessions. What do you most enjoy about counseling? Is it ever difficult to keep your work from personally affecting you?**

I do enjoy counseling, but in moderation. It is always a tremendous privilege to help people through their greatest pains and struggles. I'm an empathetic person, so I find it very easy to enter into someone's situation with them, think and feel deeply with them, and then help them pursue God. But too much of this can drain me quickly. As many counselors experience, there is a downside to being empathetic: I have a difficult time setting other people's issues aside so that I can go home lighthearted, ready to wrestle with my kids, make dinner with Jamie, or spend time with friends. Sometimes, if I glance in the rearview mirror on the way home from the office, I think I can spot a wrinkle that wasn't there that morning.

Pastors and therapists have a lot in common. I know this personally—both of my parents are psychologists. My mom and dad and I all love people and find it easy to "feel with them." But when you love people, you tend to struggle with boundaries. I find that a few simple activities help me "unplug" and transition from work to home—things such as exercising, making dinner, or fishing my way around a lake at sundown.

3. **You write that men "usually know when they've gone too far with a pursuit . . . you'll hear men frequently use the words 'obsession' and 'addiction' to describe their pursuit . . . .When someone admits to an addiction or obsession, he's admitting that he's no longer in control." Do you think there are instances when obsessive pursuits, such as hunting and sports, can be as destructive as physical addictions?**

Without minimizing the destruction of drugs and alcohol, there is no question in my mind that our pursuits can be as hurtful as our physical addictions. I have a friend who is addicted to smoking and drinking. He's also obsessed with hunting and fishing. We hunted together this past week and he told me his wife left him recently. She stopped him at the door as he was leaving to hunt moose in Alaska and said that she was "done playing second fiddle to hunting." The emotional and relational pain caused by this man's fanaticism is every bit as real and severe as the pain caused by an addiction to a drug.

4. You write candidly about your own shortcomings. Was it difficult to put your flaws down on paper? Were you at all concerned about how your readers might perceive you?

My highest goal for *Man on the Run* was not to present myself in a good light, it was to invite others to join me in the journey of making better choices. What's more, I'm soberly aware that I'm a work in progress myself. It would have been disingenuous to take the voice of a wise old sage in *Man on the Run*. (I could have perhaps gotten away with that voice, but I would've had to keep the people who are closest to me from reading the book.)

I do write and speak about my flaws at times, but I am extremely intentional about *what* and *how much* I share with others. If I share something personal or vulnerable, it's only after I've given it great thought. Authenticity is a vital part of teaching and counseling, as it is with all relationships, but I certainly don't advocate people sharing every thought and feeling they have going on inside. I believe we must be wise about the words we share.

5. **Since writing this book would you say that you've changed as a husband and father? In what areas do you feel like you still fall short? What do you feel that you're best at? How do you anticipate your role in your family changing as your children get older?**

The span of time from when I sat down to type out a proposal for *Man on the Run* to when it was published took about four years. Those were deeply formative years for me. I'm not sure how much to attribute to the writing process and how much to attribute to other relationships and events, but I'm a much more *resolved* husband and father today. I know more clearly what kind of man I want to be, and I'm finding joy in being that man.

I still fall short all the time, however. I would say that my biggest challenge is still in the area of balance. I enjoy moving at a fast pace, but this means that I need to work even harder at prioritizing and carrying out my priorities. I still go through seasons in which I don't spend as much time with Jamie, my kids, or my community of friends as I should and want to. I'm not sure

I'll ever reach "perfect status" in this area, but I do feel the need to keep growing and learning in this area of balance.

With respect to "what I feel I'm best at," I think that the people in my life know that I love them. You'd have to ask them, but I think my wife, kids, and community would say that I communicate my affection in several ways. I work hard to spend time with the people I love. I unpack my day with Jamie each evening, and our family has dinner together most nights of the week. I tuck our children into bed each night, praying with them and talking with them about the ups and downs of their days. I keep up fairly well with my closest friends and regularly communicate to them how much I value their friendship.

6. **Based on your chapter headings and the quotes you use throughout your book, you seem to have a wide and eclectic range of interest in music and books. Who are some of your favorite writers and musicians?**

In all honesty, I didn't realize how "all over the map" I was with my citations until the book was completed. This does represent me accurately. I've always appreciated art and the people who use words to create it.

With respect to music, I've always loved Van Morrison. I can remember being eight years old and putting his album *Wavelength* on my dad's turntable several times a week. I listen to a variety of genres, but I seem to gravitate toward folk or Americana. Some of my favorite musicians are Mumford and Sons, Johnny Cash, U2, Pierce Pettis, Bon Iver, Allison Krauss, João Gilberto, Charlie Peacock, Michael Card, Glen Hansard, Josh Ritter, Rich Mullins, Andrew Peterson, the Avett Brothers, and Coldplay.

With respect to authors, I have several favorites: Wendell Berry, Dallas Willard, John Piper, Eugene Peterson, Timothy Keller, Jon Krakauer, James Herriot, John Muir, Jonathan Edwards, C. S. Lewis, and J.R.R. Tolkien. Some of my favorite books are *The Count of Monte Cristo* by Alexandre Dumas, *All Creatures Great and Small* by James Herriot, and *Sherlock Holmes* by Sir Arthur Conan Doyle. I also love to read *The Jesus Storybook Bible* to my children.

7. Are you planning to write another book? Would you ever consider genres other than nonfiction?

I'm already at work on another book idea. It's a nonfiction book that deals with another frontline issue that men and their families face. I would like to venture out and write in other genres. One of my favorite genres to read is narrative nonfiction. A few of my favorite books in this genre are *The Long Walk* by Slavomir Rawicz, *Unbroken* by Laura Hillenbrand, *The Perfect Mile* by Neal Bascomb, *The Last Season* by Eric Blehm, *Into Thin Air* by Jon Krakauer, and *The Perfect Storm* by Sebastian Junger. I would enjoy the research and writing involved in telling these types of stories.

8. Have you encountered any women who have neglected their families because of their passions and pursuits in the same way that men tend to?

Yes, I have seen women chase their passions into hurtful places at times, but not nearly as often as I've watched men do it. This is a sweeping generalization, but it seems to me that women do not have the same amount of time or permission (from themselves or society) to pursue their hobbies. In general, men appear to have, or take, more opportunities to chase pursuits (such as hobbies, sports, and careers) than women today. Also, men's hobbies are often interspersed with their work, i.e., playing golf or racquetball with clients.

That being said, I believe it is possible for women to focus on one important priority to the point of hurting other people. For example, nurturing children is such a strong, driving instinct for many mothers that it can push aside the priority of being a good companion and lover to their husbands. When I counsel couples who are struggling with intimacy, I often need to challenge the wife to give more time, energy, and affection to her husband.

9. **Do you think that some people may be unwilling to commit to a church because they feel they must "follow the rules" perfectly or that they won't be accepted? How do you think people's negative perceptions of going to church can be changed?**

Being a deeply committed, integral part of a local church is difficult. And, as you suggest in your question, it's often difficult precisely because people in the church place heavy expectations and judgments upon one another's shoulders. This is tragically ironic, because life with Jesus and His people is supposed to be characterized by a "light and easy yoke" (see Matthew 11:29–30).

To be honest, I'm not exactly sure why we do this to each other in churches. My gut tells me it has something to do with trying to find our sense of self-worth and belonging in how we measure up to (against) other people. But this competitiveness is so opposed to the Gospel, which is supposed to bring us together as a church. The Gospel is the good news that we are fully worthy and that we fully belong because of the work of Jesus Christ. Because of the grace of God, we don't need to pick at each other anymore. For some reason, this is a hard truth for many churches to grasp and apply.

With respect to "changing people's impressions of church," there's only one thing that will do this: people who live in and live out the grace of God. As church leaders, it's tempting to think that a fancy sign out front, an upbeat Sunday worship service, and a hospitality bag in the foyer will encourage people to come to church. Programs, gifts, and marketing strategies do not hold the power to draw and keep people in a local church—the power is found in the message that we can be forgiven and perfectly accepted by God and His people because of the work of Christ. People who enjoy the grace of God, and invite others to do the same, change perceptions. It's really that simple.

10. **In describing the process a person must go through to make a significant life change, you write that "it's typically not a fun experience for the man. Much like having a boil scraped off or a tooth extracted, the transformation of our hearts is not fun." Why**

is it often so painful to experience change, even though life after the change can be so much better? Why do you think we are conditioned to fear change?

The heart is like a rusty old wheel on an abandoned tractor; it doesn't change quickly. It's been my experience that most life-changing experiences begin with pain—either a painful situation or a painful confession or both. I wish it didn't have to work this way—I don't want anyone I love to go through pain—but C. S. Lewis appears to be right when he said that "pain is God's megaphone to rouse a deaf world."

We're conditioned to fear change because we're uncomfortable with pain. And change is rarely accomplished without pain. Changing jobs or moving invites the emotional pain of saying good-bye. Getting married or having children brings with it the relational pain of accommodation. Confessing our sins, seeking help, and changing our commitments and practices often require the pain of humility and brokenness. I wrote *Man on the Run* to encourage men to see that the pleasure on the back end is worth the pain of change.

11. **When writing this book, did you consider your audience to be primarily men, or would you say it's aimed**

at both men and women? Did you rely heavily on input from both men and women?

I wrote *Man on the Run* for both men and women. Although I primarily discuss men and their issues in this book, I'm assuming that more women than men will read these pages. It's been my experience that women put a lot of relational and intellectual energy into thinking deeply about the men in their lives (sons, fathers, husbands, and friends). I wanted to write in such a way that men could find themselves in these pages, but also so that women felt invited into the dialogue. I did this because both men and women are vital to the story of a man living well.

I have several strong, intelligent women in my life who have helped shape and guide my deepest beliefs and values. My wife, mother, mother-in-law, agent, and a couple close family friends have interacted with the ideas I discuss in *Man on the Run*. They have corrected and redirected me at times. I obviously have some great men in my life who have shaped my thinking, but it has largely been the women in my life who have helped me understand both men and women. I believe that men live their best lives when they respect, honor, and listen to the women in their lives.

12. If your readers could take away only one thing from this book, what would you say is the most important message?

There is nothing more amazing, more exhilarating, more demanding, and more challenging than living in a personal relationship with Jesus Christ. Life is short, so the sooner a person tastes and sees that the Lord is good, the sooner he or she can get on with the business of really living.